ANDY MCILREE

Seeing the Bride in the Song of Songs

HAYES
PRESS Christian Publisher

First edition

This book was professionally typeset on Reedsy.
Find out more at reedsy.com

"My beloved put in his hand by the hole of the door, and my heart was moved for him."

Song of Solomon 5:4 RV

Contents

1

INTRODUCTION

As we found in our previous book on 'Women God Moved,' God chooses His women well, and there is no higher honour or place He could give them, than to make them the means of 'Seeing the Bride in all the Scriptures.' As each Christian woman reads her Bible, she will find that the God who made Woman elevates women. In Genesis 1:27,28, Eve shared equality with Adam by being made in the image of God, then she shared in communion with God when He blessed them, and authority from God when He *"said to them … have dominion over … every living thing that moves on the earth."* From then on, there is a Bible-wide harvest of women who yielded fruitful service to God, so, overall, we are left in no doubt that her role is *of* God, *with* God, *from* God, and *to* God, meaning she is neither secondary nor inferior.

He works similarly with men, of course, and gives different commendations to them, each worth having, yet one seems to stand out above the others. We find it among a seemingly endless list of names in the opening chapters of 1 Chronicles. It begins with Adam and ultimately comes to the family of Asher at the end of chapter 7. It's been worth wading through and waiting for, while there are men who are heads, mighty and chief, and some accredited as famous, only the children of Asher are called *"choice."* Does it matter? Oh, yes! For the little Hebrew word *b-ᵉrūrīm* is used elsewhere in the Old Testament to describe arrows that were made bright,[1] and of one in particular that is *"a polished shaft."*[2] Isaiah was speaking of the Lord Jesus Himself, the only completely pure, perfectly bright and polished Servant of God who was the outshining of His glory.[3]

What an honour, then, to be described as "choice"! But among all the sons of Asher, God includes two special names: *"their sister Serah"* and *"their sister Shua."* How lovely is that? It would appear their names could mean 'superfluous' and 'wealth,' a superfluity and wealth in ways that mattered to God. Choice women! Sister, let this be your ambition. Leave it to others to seek fame and power and the chief places. Go after being *"choice"* and He will take care of the rest.

Now as we set out to consider another of God's literary masterpieces in the beauties of 'The Song of Songs,' we will see how He caused this particular woman to depict something very special that He had in mind. God always calls and leads a singing people, so it's not accidental that this part of His Word was composed as a song. How noticeable it is, that there were no songs in Genesis, as He opened up a way back to Himself for fallen man! The blight of Eden's sin casts its long, dark shadow throughout its fifty chapters: firstly, on a personal level with murderous Cain in chapter 4, and then with other individuals who fathered ungodly nations. Chapter 10 lists those that came from Noah's three sons, many of whom became fierce enemies of the people of God, as were Moab and Ammon who were spawned in chapter 19:36-38 from Lot's shameful behaviour with his daughters. Amid all that darkness, God was shining His light that beamed through the line of Abraham, Isaac and Jacob until, at last, it was diffused in twelve sons from whom would come the

2

holy nation of Israel. Yes, He was standing "within the shadow, keeping watch above his own."[4] No wonder James Russell Lowell went on to write:

> Once to every man and nation
> Comes the moment to decide,
> In the strife of Truth with Falsehood,
> For the good or evil side;
> Some great cause, God's new Messiah,
> Offering each the bloom or blight,
> Parts the goats upon the left hand,
> And the sheep upon the right,
> And the choice goes by forever
> 'Twixt that darkness and that light.

Exodus 12 was such a moment. Suddenly, while there was darkness that could be felt among the Egyptians, *"all the children of Israel had light in their dwellings."* [5] Under the good hand of the God of love, light and life, they were about to discover all three through the wonder of their redemption provided through the blood of the Passover lamb. Making their way out through blood-stained portals and lintels, Egypt's doors were shut behind them and they went forward to discover that the same great God had opened a door through the Red Sea for them. With walls of water on either side, not bricks and straw,[6] and the dry seabed as their floor, they arrived in triumph on the other side by the same divine power promised to the church in Philadelphia in Revelation 3:8, *"I have set before you an open door, and no one can shut it."* He had closed a door that no one could open, and opened a door that no one could close. It was then they sang!

The Song of Moses

Silence was broken. For the first time on earth the people of God sang, and it was no ordinary song! Was it spontaneous? Was Moses the composer? At such a time of heightened praise, probably, 'Yes.' But the One who caused their praise, the provider of the lamb, the opener and closer of doors, was He not also the Inspirer of the song? In a unique chorus, it was if He had caused the tongue of the dumb to sing,[7] and He will never forget it. In the harmony that belongs to Scripture, it will be sung again. Having found it recorded in the fifteenth chapter of the second book in our Bible, we find it again in the fifteenth chapter of the last book. It was first sung at the beginning of their walk as the redeemed on earth, and it will be sung again at the end of their walk on earth when the redeemed from the great tribulation sing it in heaven. Commenting on both, it has been well said, "The song of Moses was sung at the Red Sea, the song of the Lamb is sung at the crystal sea; the song of Moses was a song of triumph over Egypt, the song of the Lamb is a song of triumph over Babylon; the song of Moses told how God brought His people out, the song of the Lamb tells how God brings His people in; the song of Moses was the first song of Scripture, the song of the Lamb is the last. The song of Moses commemorated the execution of the foe, the expectation of the saints, and the exaltation of the Lord; the song of the Lamb deals with the same three themes."[8]

Between these two great occasions, it has become customary for the Song of Solomon to be read in synagogues each year at Passover time and, and they attach a high regard to it in its place among the Kethuvim (The Writings) of the Tanakh. However, traditionally, Jews were not allowed to read it until they were thirty years old. James Durham confirms this on page 42 of his treasured commentary: "It is true, this, and some other scriptures were of old restrained by the Jews, from the younger sort, that none should read them, but those who were at thirty years of age." More recently, it has been said that The Song is for private meditation, not for public ministry. Whether in Old Testament or New Testament days, there is no Scriptural warrant for such impositions, though, like any part of God's Word, divine revelation calls for spiritual discernment and care. We can set aside such restrictions, claiming it where it so rightly belongs among the inspired pages of God's Word.[9] Testimony also is borne to this in early Jewish writing: "No Israelite has ever disputed the canonicity of the Song of Songs. No day in the whole history of the world is of so much worth as the one in which the Song of Songs was given to Israel; for all the Scriptures are holy, but the Song of Songs is most holy" (R. Akiba in the Mishna Yadim, section iii. 5).

More recently, Rabbi Leah Richman [Director of Adult Learning, Center for the Advancement of Jewish Education (Miami)] has written: "The Song of Songs or the Song of Solomon which it is also called, is one of the five scrolls read on various holidays throughout the year. The entire book is a series of love songs in poetic form. The book is unique in the books of the Bible in that not only does it not mention G-d, it also doesn't deal with religious themes explicitly. While the book of Esther also fails to mention G-d, the spirit of nationalism and the Jewish people pervades the book in a way which is lacking here.

But back to our topic: why do we read this book on Passover and what can we learn from the Passover story by reading the Song of Songs? One explanation is that the Song of Songs is really an allegory for the love of G-d for the people Israel. Since the story of the Exodus is also the beginning of the love relationship between G-d and Israel, Passover is an appropriate time to learn about this love. The lover in the song is taken to be G-d, and the beloved is the people Israel. This allegorical reading was widespread among the rabbis in our tradition by the 1st century CE. The song was ascribed to King Solomon because of the few times his name is mentioned in the book and because of its references to a king. The strongest support for the allegorical interpretation comes from Rabbi Akiba who said this book was the holiest among all of the writings. The song has also been variously interpreted through the Christian church, as a drama, as a cultic liturgy, or on its literal level as a secular love song. In the allegorical interpretation however, we can learn more deeply about the love of G-d for Israel which is our connection to the Passover story."

Interpreting the Song

We thought of this briefly in the fourth chapter of the previous book in the series 'Women God Moved' when we looked at the Shulamite of the Song. We need to enquire who the couple and their song represent. Various suggestions have been made regarding different ways of interpreting and applying it:

> a) The individual Jew's personal relationship with God;
> b) Israel's collective national relationship with God;
> c) The individual believer's relationship with Christ;
> d) The church - the body's relationship with Christ;
> e) It can be used for counselling Christian couples.

The present writer believes that Rabbi Leah Richman is right when she indicates that the primary application is to Israel's collective relationship with God. If not, why would it be in the Old Testament canon of Scripture? As with any portion of God's Word, we need to determine the primary application before attempting to draw any parallel lessons for ourselves. Otherwise, we will quickly become tangled in our own thinking if all we do is read an Old Testament portion and ask, "What's in it for me?"

Bearing in mind, that *"whatever things were written before were written for our learning, that we through patience and comfort of the Scriptures might have hope,"*[10] we may safely conclude that 'The Song' holds valuable lessons for (c) and (d). Even so, it is hardly possible that divine inspiration caused such beautiful Hebrew poetry to be written mainly for such a man-centred purpose as the last possibility. So it's better that we allow its language to lift our thoughts to see God being exalted in His relationship with His people, Israel, and how His Son may be exalted as we draw lessons that relate to our walk with Him.

Imagery

In spite of having such a range of possible interpretations, there's no need to be afraid of The Song for it's a very human book, and very devotional. Its pages are like unsealing a sequence of love letters, not sentimental rhetoric. *"The heart knows its own bitterness"*[11]; it knows its own affections too. The Song is a successful attempt by a young couple to express this in words and behaviour. Their imagery isn't an unusual way of doing this. Although it may seem odd to us, they would interpret and properly understand the wholesome appreciation that each had for the other. In our own way, we speak descriptively of people and it's quite common to say that someone has a heart of gold, eyes like a hawk, or a brass neck.

The bride speaks appreciatively of her bridegroom, and the Song develops like sharing their hearts' secrets. The imagery tends to be very descriptive and not always straightforward for us to understand. However, it is clear that they knew what each other meant. If we try to think of what the imagery is naturally, we can think of how they were applying it to one another and, then, how we can apply it to our own relationship with our Lord and Saviour.

She starts off by saying, *"Your name is ointment poured forth,"*[12] by which she invites us to think of the value, fragrance, soothing and healing associated with ointment. Even so, there is no shortage of it for it is unsparingly "poured forth" to show its generous supply. He is never meagre or inadequate in what he gives, nor is his impress on her heart and mind ever scant or insufficient. No, he empties that she might be filled, he is selfless in his blessings and benefits, and his renown clings to her as fragrance does to clothing and curtains. It is obvious that the very thought of his name made her aware of all these aspects of his character, like the ingredients of ointment, as if she were inhaling the compounded value of his person. She took in what he poured out, and she made no secret of the fact that he was desirable. Using the imagery, she would have sensed the beneficial healing effect that he had on their friendship, and she would bear the fragrance that was made totally available to her so that her life might be filled by its preciousness.

From this lovely beginning of imagery language, we can already enjoy its application to ourselves as we think of the worthiest Name we know. What do we think when the Name of Jesus is mentioned? Does His identity evoke all the ingredient characteristics of His Person? He wants us to experience His friendship[13], fragrance[14] and His fulness[15], so *"He poured out His soul unto death"*[16] to make it possible. Having already *"emptied Himself"*[17] by leaving behind the glory He had in the presence of His God and Father, he humbled Himself to the extent that on the cross He was *"poured out like water."*[18] He knew the full cost of being emptied that we might know the joy of being filled. On His return to his Father's side, God *"poured out"* the gift of the Holy Spirit[19] at Pentecost, then He *"poured out"* the Holy Spirit on us when we believed,[20] and the

Holy Spirit graciously *"poured out"* God's love into our hearts.[21] We have every reason to say, "Jesus, You are everything to me." But when last did we say it?

The unusual imagery continues when she says, *"Sustain me with cakes of raisins, refresh me with apples,"*[22] and it's evident that we are not intended to take these literally or conclude that Christians should keep vines and orchards to maintain a full supply of fruit. Raisins come from the vine, apples from the apple tree, and both tell of the fruitfulness of her beloved. She has just referred to him as being *"Like an apple tree among the trees of the wood,"* by which she meant his benefits were not only available, but accessible. Now she was talking his language for his knowledge of trees was one of Solomon's specialities *"from the cedar tree of Lebanon even to the hyssop that springs out of the wall."*[23] Well might Psalm 116:7 have been spoken by her regarding the blessing of time spent in his company: *"Return to your rest, O my soul, for the LORD has dealt bountifully with you."* It certainly ought to have reflected Israel's appreciation of God in His goodness to her as a nation, but, like the bride, she struggled to do this and would have to remind herself to say, as David did in Psalm 103:2, *"Bless the LORD, O my soul, and forget not all His benefits."*

As we apply this to the Person of Christ, we know that all our fruitfulness comes from Him[24] for only by abiding in Him can we bear *"fruit ... more fruit"* and *"much fruit."*[25] The purpose of this study is not to attempt a verse-by-verse consideration of the Song, but to trace some of the themes that are developed during the course of its eight chapters.

CHRIST, MY BELOVED

"A bundle of myrrh[26] *is my beloved to me, that lies all night between my breasts. My beloved is to me a cluster of henna*[27] *blossoms in the vineyards of En Gedi"* (Song of Songs 1:13,14)

He is, and was, and ever He will be
A presence near, and ever real to me;
By day and night, like myrrh and henna flowers,
He brings His fragrance to those darkest hours.

From darkness, darker than we ever know, (Matt.27:45)
From grief much deeper than we ever show, (Matt.26:38)
There came the sweetest fragrance ever known (Eph.5:1,2)
As on the cross He suffered for His own. (1 Pet.3:18)

Such bitterness from sour, embittered men
Swept over Him again, and then again;
Yet nought compared with every wrath-filled wave (Ps.42:7; 88:7)
The Saviour bore for those He came to save.

Within the travail of His outpoured soul, (Is.53:11 KJV)
And through the blood that makes the outcast whole, (1 Pet.1:18,19)
Redemption's price was paid, the ransom given, (Ps.49:8)
That takes dead men from sin and gives them life – and heaven.

And is the reason for his death now seen
By your own heart in your own need of Him?
Is it the place where Jesus now belongs,
The fragrance of your life, your Song of songs?

2

THE SONG OF SONGS

"The song of songs, which is Solomon's.
Let him kiss me with the kisses of his mouth—
For your love is better than wine.
Because of the fragrance of your good ointments,
Your name is ointment poured forth;
Therefore the virgins love you.
Draw me away!
We will run after you."
(Song of Songs 1:1-4)

* * *

Solomon was a prolific writer. We learn from 1 Kings 4:32 that he composed one thousand and five songs and compiled three thousand proverbs, though it makes no mention of his third book, Ecclesiastes. The Old Testament contains valuable literary reminders of particular stages in his life: The Song, probably written as a young man; the Proverbs, when he was middle-aged; and the absence of any mention of Ecclesiastes helps to indicate that he wrote it in his latter years.

The superlative quality of this short book is captured in its opening words in Hebrew *shīr hashīrīm*. Coupling the same noun, singular beside plural, was the normal way of emphasising such uniqueness. For example, in:

- Genesis 9:25 – Noah cursed his grandson, Canaan, by calling him *"a servant of servants"* meaning *"the lowest of slaves"* (NIV);
- Exodus 29:37 – the Hebrew phrase for *"most holy"* means *"holy of holies"*;
- Deuteronomy 10:14 – Here *"the highest heavens"* is a translation of *"the heaven of heavens"*;
- Ezra 7:12 – the title *"king of kings"* infers the greatest king;
- Ecclesiastes 1:2 – in this verse, *"vanity of vanities"* is translated as *"utterly meaningless"* in the NIV.

The exception is found in references to the *"God of gods,"*[1] which, still with singular alongside plural, doesn't infer that He is greater than, or the greatest of, other gods. In this case, He alone is the supreme, living, all-powerful One, while all gods are lifeless and powerless. Unlike all the others, it's not a statement of degree here, but His singular claim to Deity, since only He is God. So, while it is appropriate to speak of the lowest servant, the holiest place, the highest heavens, the greatest king, and the vainest vanity, it is completely inappropriate to think of God as greatest in the context of other gods, since none is great or greater than another. The contrast is immeasurable: we are the work of His hands,[2] and they are the work of men's hands.[3]

The Song of Songs

Questions immediately come to mind. The Song of songs, the best of songs, by whose assessment? Compared to what other songs? Are they all the songs of Scripture or confined to the one thousand and five written by Solomon? Is it possible that the Inspirer who has included it among the holy writings would grade it higher than other songs in His inspired Word? It seems unlikely, for would He ever exalt one Gospel record over another? Would He take their four themes of King, Servant, Man and God, and prefer one over another? Or, for that matter, His prophets: would He ever take what He gave them to say and then announce one as greater or greatest? Even among the Psalms, is there the slightest possibility that He would elevate one as chief among the one hundred and fifty?

Undoubtedly, He is the assessor of this Song, since *"The song of songs, which is Solomon's"* was written by His inspiration. It would hardly be profitable to conclude that He is the Assessor of His own songs, since there could never be levels or degrees of inspiration. It is much more likely that He would prize one of Solomon's, because He had inspired it to convey a much deeper meaning than the wise man could ever attach to his bridal relationship. We therefore treat it as the best of his songs, since it truly is from his penmanship and composition, but from God's purpose, inspiration and application.

The Song therefore comes to us through the heart of Solomon as penman, not to show the limitations of his own affections and appeal, but to help us see into the heart of God as provider. An early Scottish writer noted this and added, "Nor is there need to enquire who was the penman of it, it being clear that Solomon who was furnished with wisdom and understanding ... is honoured to be the Amanuensis of the

Holy Ghost, in putting this Song upon record."[4] In spite of his failings, he takes his place among the honoured rank of those men who *"spoke as they were moved by the Holy Spirit."*[5]

What we have, then, in these eight chapters is the supremacy of God, clothed in His fervency and intimacy. Even under Law, His working with His people had much grace blended with it; and, as His Spirit applies the lessons we draw to our walk with our Saviour, He will share with us something from *"the exceeding riches of His grace in his kindness toward us in Christ."*[6] God has included this Song in His Word for our good, and we should allow the Holy Spirit to interpret and apply it richly to our Christian lives. By His help, we will trace the beauties of this allegory until truths are formed that will shape the course of our spiritual will and walk.

It is to be expected that, since God the Father and God the Son are identical in divine nature, Their affections will be expressed in like tenderness. This being so, the expressions in the Song can readily be taken as God's endearments toward the people He loves, Israel, and easily transferred to the love-bond between the Lord Jesus Christ and His own. It would seem apparent that the Father would draw a similar response from His bride, Israel, as Christ expects from His, the church. By this, we mean the evidence of redemption and the fruit of righteousness.

Believer's Needs

With the title of the song announced in the opening verse – *"The song of songs, which is Solomon's"* – the Shulamite's bridal longings are announced in terms of utter dependence and fitting impatience that can immediately be recognised and applied by followers of the Lord Jesus

Christ. It was as if she were voicing a list of believer's needs.

- in chapter 1:2, Kiss me - **AFFECTION**;
- in chapter 1:4, Draw me - **ATTRACTION**;
- in chapter 1:7, Tell me - **INSTRUCTION**;
- in chapter 2:4, Brought me - **INTENTION**;
- in chapter 2:5, Sustain me - **PROVISION**;
- in chapter 2:5, Refresh me - **RESTORATION**;
- in chapter 2:6, Embraces me - **PROTECTION**.

There is an unknown background to the opening of the Song, but, whatever prior contact or conversation there may have been, her heart was at bursting point. This is more than evident in her first urgent request, which shows the closeness of the relationship she desires.

*Affection

The closeness of the relationship is shown in verse 2, but she didn't say, "Let me kiss him." By dwelling on what she needed from him, rather than what he needed from her, she continued to emphasise his pre-eminence. She spoke of undivided, uncontended, unshared love, and by saying, "Let him," she was giving him permission to claim her affections. Their closeness is an example of God's openness with Moses of whom He said, *"I speak with him face to face."*[7] Samuel's closeness to God is another lovely example for *"the LORD was with him and let none of his words fall to the ground."*[8] It also urges us to own Christ in a first-love relationship,[9] not sharing our love, not loving self or loving the world for it's possible to be so divided in our affection that we become no more than spiritual flirts! In contrast to such a possibility, Paul urged the Colossians to *"set* [their] *affection on things above,"*[10] with all the implications of their minds having the inner focus that is the upward effect of putting on love.[11]

Sometimes, we speak about a person's heart being in the right place, by which we mean they are genuinely committed to someone or something. For Solomon's father, David, it meant both for he *"set* [his] *affection on the house of* [his] *God."*[12] He is a real example for us, too, of course, for only those who love the God of their salvation can truly be devoted to Him in service. How futile it is, if we try to serve Him when our hearts are not in it. David put it a different way when he prayed, *"O Lord, open my lips, and my mouth shall show forth Your praise."*[13] We can pray this, too: and then add, "Let Him!"

The real value of a personal relationship with Christ depends upon absorbing His affection, not upon Him absorbing ours. He can live without mine, but I cannot live without His. It was His love for us that started the relationship in the first place,[14] and we love in return. And then obedience flows from our love to Him.[15] She began by saying, "Let him." This means she was allowing him, and indicates her submissiveness. But what is submission? Does it mean taking second place, being inferior, or throwing your own will out of the window? No, real submission means yielding to love through love. It is the willingness to own the will of the one who seeks our best. Willingness comes from love, so does giving, not from force! This is shown in Ephesians 5:23-25. The wife subjects herself to her husband, and he has to love her *"just as Christ also loved the church and gave Himself for her."* The words "just as" mean that He loved the church sacrificially, through His cross. So, the husband has not to rule like a despot and browbeat his wife into submission. It's not the wrestling ring type of submission that he wants. That would be failure in his part, for he also is called to submit to the mind of Christ. Both have to show Christlikeness in their actions, and this will reveal how they own the Headship of Christ as a couple.

"Let him kiss me" is a face-to-face experience, nothing between, and never by turning our backs on Him. Our spiritual excitement about our Saviour's love should have an effect on others, as it did for the bride in the Song. Listen to the daughters of Jerusalem as they ask her, *"Where has your beloved gone, O fairest among women? Where has your beloved turned aside, that we may seek him with you?*[16] They had already plied her with another double question, but on that occasion it was, *"What is your beloved more than another beloved, O fairest of women? What is your beloved more than another beloved, that you so charge us?"*[17] She gave them such a good answer to their "What?" that they also wanted to know "Where?" Do you feel ready for such questions? Peter prepares us, and his advice is, *"But in your hearts set apart Christ as Lord. Always be prepared to give an answer to everyone who asks you to give the reason for the hope you have. But do this with gentleness and respect."*[18]

*Attraction

Naturally speaking, we are attracted to a partner through such things as nature, features and manner. It was the same with the bride. She could describe him so accurately. When her friends asked her, "What?" she mentioned six things about him without going below the neck: head, hair, eyes, cheeks, lips, and mouth.[19] Could we give such a detailed description of the Saviour based on how He is seen in the Scriptures? Their questions focused on "Where?" and "What?" but, in chapter 3:6, her own question concentrated on "Who?" She must be satisfied with knowing who he is, as well as knowing where and what he is, and it's the same with us and the Saviour. We must know who He is, and the more we know the better we will be at showing where and what He is!

She also wanted to be drawn. Her words, "Draw me", could be translated "Develop me," and there's no doubt, if we will allow the Lord to draw us and offer no resistance, spiritual development will take place. But He won't drag us! Love draws. It doesn't drive. It constrains, but doesn't compel. She wanted to be drawn away from independence to dependence. Which do we prefer? If we ask to be drawn, we are admitting that there is a distance between ourselves and Him. If so, it is good to admit it when there is. We should feel in partnership with Him, and that means closeness. And we should be in partnership with one another - *"We will run after you."*[20] Each one of us should feel that he or she is a meaningful part of the church, for we have known God's drawing power.[21]

If, then, we are drawn by Him and to Him, we ought to be drawn to one another! And there may be tough times when we will value being drawn up by one another as Jeremiah was.[22] We can learn a lot from chapter 1:4 that will help to promote togetherness – *"We will run … We will be glad … We will remember your love."* Her excitement about his love affected others. It was spontaneous and contagious. What about ours? Can we honestly say that our love is genuine – no hypocrisy, no play-acting or going through the motions. We need to be upright. When asked, "Do you love Him? we should be able to say, "Rightly do they love you."

*Instruction

Chapter 1:7 makes it plain that she wanted to know some guidance from the one who was her soul-love, and, since it also shows that she didn't want to be with anyone else, it's equally clear that he was her sole-love. As Christians, we each have to ask ourselves, "Is Christ my soul-love and my sole-love?" Do we have such singleness of heart that we are ready to ask for His instruction? The bride said, "Tell me … where," and this suggests certain kinds of instruction. First of all, it implies direction. Secondly, the word "Tell" implies explanation and exposition. That is,

18

to teach in such a way that the instruction is laid out step by step. In Mark 4:34, the Lord expounded everything to His disciples and it says that He did it privately. Exposition is for those who have soul-love, who want to spend time with their Saviour in the Word because they want to follow Him.

It is interesting to see in Dr. Strong's concordance that the word "Tell" is closely associated with a Hebrew word which means "counterpart, or a mate." This is a vivid word picture, which fits the close tie between bride and bridegroom: each being the counterpart of the other, and between us and Christ. Receiving instruction is part of the joy of our one-to-One relationship with Him, and not hungering for it shows there is something seriously wrong. Our attitude to receiving spiritual guidance from Him can be summed up in the following scriptures: *"I will hear what God the LORD will speak, for He will speak peace to His people and to His saints. Teach me Your way, O LORD; I will walk in Your truth; unite my heart to fear Your name."* [23]

*Intention

The word *yātsā'* from which we get our word *"Follow"* in chapter 1:8 is sometimes translated as *"bring out"*[24] and leads on to *"He brought me"* in chapter 2:4, which can be translated as *"bring into."*[25] So, chapter 1 is going it alone; chapter 2 is going together. There is a sense of fellowship in the second, and the distance between bridegroom and bride has disappeared for the time being! The lesson is, of course, that before she could be brought in she had to be brought out, and this is something the children of Israel could say that God did for them when *"He brought us out from there, that He might bring us in."*[26] Being brought out of bondage in Egypt must precede being brought into Canaan; and, for us, being brought out of the bondage of our sin must precede being brought into Christ.

Being *brought out* is cause for praise. Being brought in allows us to have an outlet for praise. The bride was brought into his *"banqueting house"* or *"house of wine."* This seems to indicate the place where joy can be shared and expressed. Each had placed the other's love above the joy associated with wine,[27] but *"the house of wine"* was a place of joyful communion, and that's what we should have in the service of the Lord.

*Provision and restoration

"Sustain me" and *"Refresh me"* reveal her need of being supported and refreshed, but these are not the blessings of a casual acquaintance or a haphazard relationship. The thought of being sustained is translated in Psalm 88:7 as *"lies heavy,"* and in Leviticus 16:21 as *"lay"* where hands leaned on the head of the sacrifice. To be stayed means a total sense of dependence; putting full reliance on her beloved. These verses all draw on the word *sāmak*, and so also does Isaiah 26:3 – *"You will keep him in perfect peace, whose mind is stayed on You, because he trusts in You."* This means total support from Him, and total dependence from us! Being comforted by the bridegroom reminds us that the Lord is our true Comforter, as well as the Holy Spirit and the Father.[28]

*Protection

As we bring all these aspects of her appeal together we will notice how all-encompassing they are of her as a person. She longs to be embraced, not merely held, but securely clasped by him. But this is only one feature of the closeness she desires. Overall, she is defining what it means to experience what Hebrews 5:14 says about those who *"have their senses exercised."* Reference is made to:

- her **sight**: *"You have dove's eyes"* (1:15);
- her **hearing**: by saying, *"Tell me"* (1:7);
- her **taste**: *"Your love is better than wine"* (1:2; 2:3);
- her **smell**: *"The fragrance of your good ointments"* (1:3);
- her **touch**: *"His right hand embraces me"* (2:6).

Summary

Affection, attraction, instruction, intention, provision, restoration and protection: all these blessings from being in the presence of her beloved were accompanied by three promises from her:

1. We will run after you;
2. We will be glad and rejoice in you;
3. We will remember (make mention RV) your love.

Like her, we should make a threefold vow: to follow, to rejoice, and to testify.

STILL, STILL WITH THEE

Still, still with Thee, when purple morning breaketh,
When the bird waketh, and the shadows flee;
Fairer than morning, lovelier than daylight,
Dawns the sweet consciousness, I am with Thee.

Alone with Thee, amid the mystic shadows,
The solemn hush of nature newly born;
Alone with Thee in breathless adoration,
In the calm dew and freshness of the morn.

As in the dawning o'er the waveless ocean

The image of the morning star doth rest,
So in the stillness Thou beholdest only
Thine image in the waters of my breast.

Still, still with Thee, as to each newborn morning,
A fresh and solemn splendor still is given,
So does this blessèd consciousness, awaking,
Breathe each day nearness unto Thee and Heaven.

When sinks the soul, subdued by toil, to slumber,
Its closing eye looks up to Thee in prayer;
Sweet the repose beneath the wings o'ershading,
But sweeter still to wake and find Thee there.

So shall it be at last, in that bright morning,
When the soul waketh and life's shadows flee;
O in that hour, fairer than daylight dawning,
Shall rise the glorious thought, I am with Thee
(Harriet Beecher Stowe)

3

SHADOWS

"Tell me ... where you feed your flock,
where you make it rest at noon.
If you do not know, O fairest among women,
Follow in the footsteps of the flock ...
I sat down in his shade with great delight,
and his fruit was sweet to my taste.
Until the day breaks and the shadows flee away,
turn my beloved, and be like a gazelle or a young stag
upon the mountains of Bether.
Until the day breaks and the shadows flee away,
I will go my way to the mountain of myrrh
and to the hill of frankincense."
(Song of Songs 1:7, 8; 2:3, 17; 4:6,7)

* * *

Among the uppermost considerations that weighed in the bride's mind was this - she wanted to be assured of her beloved's pastoral care. Provision and attention are vital aspects of a shepherd's work, and the state of the flock is a good indication of his watchfulness and skill. The word *"make"* never implies force, rather it proves his ability to ensure that all conditions are right and best suited to the sheep. No shepherd can force sheep to lie down. Before they will settle, they need to be fed, watered, free of sore feet, and clear of fears or threat of predators. The shepherd brings his sheep into such a state by making every unsettling hazard disappear. When he actively makes this condition, he effectively *"causes"* his sheep to lie down. He has done everything that is necessary. This is the spiritual skill that David recognised in God when he said, *"The LORD is my shepherd; I shall not want. He makes me to lie down in green pastures."*[1] The whole psalm outlines the proper God-given conditions that allowed him to be at rest, and our Good Shepherd has done the same for all who come to him for rest.[2]

If you do not know ...

In spiritual things, ignorance is not bliss! We have thought about the questions, *"Where? What?"* and *"Who?"*, but before any of these was asked she began by asking, *"Why?"* She wanted to get an answer that would get to the bottom of her doubts and remove her uncertainty. Otherwise, she wanted to know why she should act like an unwanted, discredited woman whose face needed to be hidden.[3] The beloved was direct. He could simply have told her where he was, but he didn't. Notice what he said: *"If you do not know."* The answer to her predicament lay somewhere in what she didn't know, and in why she didn't know it. Did the Lord not do the same with the woman at the well? Having just fired her first question at Him, *"How?"*, His reply was, *"If you knew."*[4] Even when He gave His full answer, she was ready with another two questions, both confirming how little she really knew, but his gracious answers led her on to response, request, and recognition of Himself.

By similar means, He gathers our questions, too, and answers them in His own perfect way. May He never say of us what He said of Israel through Hosea 4:6, *"My people are destroyed for lack of knowledge"* and through Isaiah 5:13, *"My people have gone into captivity, because they have no knowledge."*

> All your questions large and deep,
> All the open thoughts of youth,
> Bring to Him, and you shall reap
> All the harvest of His truth.
> (C.E. Mudie)

From the unspoken past of their friendship's beginning, there was something the Shulamite needed to address, and evidently he hit the nail on the head. By adding, *"Follow in the footsteps of the flock,"* he really was telling her – and she had asked to be told! – if you had been following, you would have known. This is a major lesson for us all, especially if we want to be moved. The secret of finding the presence of the beloved, for her and for us, lies in following the flock. They will be where He is, and then we will discover that where they are, He is! Sheep invariably leave a track on the land, and the shepherd goes first. The sheep didn't follow a track, they followed their shepherd. He went first, so that, when she followed their "heels," she knew she was following his steps.[5] By being such a follower she also began to hone her own shepherding skills, as she learned to *"feed* [her own] *little goats beside the shepherds' tents.'*

In the blistering heat of the day, *"at noon,"* shepherds set up their tents as places of shade, so it was a case of being nearer to the shepherd, nearer to the shade. This is the first of the shadows in the Song, a resting-place for the flock. How wonderful to know that, *"We are His people and the sheep of His pasture,"*[6] and *"The LORD is your shade."*[7] It

25

also was the place of closest observation for the young of the flock. A similar principle applies at home here on the farm: one smaller field is sectioned off from all the others as a 'lambing park.' It is nearest to the farmhouse, therefore nearest to the place of immediate attention.

I sat down in his shade with great delight.

If the shadow indicates the place of nearness, and conveys thoughts of protection and defence, sitting down is a picture of her unchallenged commitment. The word *"sat"* means to settle down in such a way as to be married to the spot; that is, in the shade, and it reveals her inner sense of stillness, and willingness to be settled with him. The psalmist seemed to have these thoughts in mind when he drew from the same words in Psalm 91:1 – *"He who dwells* [sits down] *in the secret place of the Most High shall abide* [stay the night] *under the shadow of the Almighty."* How blessed we are, that we can combine both settings, noon and night, and have no need ever to feel unsettled or to leave the shaded safety of His presence.

There was no discomfort or unease in his presence, in the place of fulfilled desire. At this early stage she was reciprocating, in such a responsive and spontaneous way, the love of his heart toward her. Her words were like the anticipated echo of his words, *"How fair and how pleasant you are, O love, with your delights!"*[8] And they remind us of Psalm 37:4, *"Delight yourself also in the LORD, and He shall give you the desires of your heart."*

Our glorious Bridegroom has brought us into the place of eternally settled rest for the One who shone upon *"those who sit in darkness and the shadow of death"*[9] has shone into our hearts. Praise His Name! Right from our new birth He has given us His Holy Spirit as the *"guarantee,"*[10] our *arrhabōn* - the engagement ring and pledge of all that He has prepared for them that love Him. If this is what the engagement is like, what will the marriage of the Lamb be like above?

And his fruit was sweet to my taste.

How she enjoyed her beloved when she was ready to sit down! The problem was, she wasn't always in a state of readiness, and neither are we. The demands of a busy life, and giving priority to other things, deprive us from discovering, as she did, that his fruit was *"sweet."* It's a word that comes from the thought of sucking and relishing. This was the unhurried, moment by moment enjoyment of himself, whenever she presented herself in his company with the pleasure that belongs to those who say, *"Oh, taste and see that the LORD is good."*[11] What joy and utter satisfaction we have, once we have *"tasted that the Lord is gracious."*[12] But we are seriously missing out if the Provider of fruit isn't also our Producer of fruit.

It's not often that God says something three times in His word, but when He does we should take special notice of it. He often says something twice, whether in the repetition of someone's name, by repeating a statement or by speaking through one of His prophets for a second time. David gives an example of the first in Psalm 62:11 – *"God has spoken once, twice I have heard this: that power belongs to God."* Abraham, Jacob, Moses, Samuel, Martha, Simon, and Saul, are seven whose names were repeated;[13] and Abraham, David, Jeremiah, Jonah and Haggai are among those to whom God spoke a second time.[14]

When it comes to something said three times, our minds may turn to Samuel, Jesus and Peter.[15] To them, we can add Amos, the writer of Hebrews, and James for they all refer to *"the fruit of righteousness,"*[16] though for very different reasons. Amos condemns those who take it as the goodness of God and turn it into poisonous effects on others. By contrast, Hebrews presents the peace and prosperity that comes to those who train themselves to live in its godly standard; and James gives the maxim that the right seed sown in the right way in the right place, will produce a harvest that is right for God.

One of the beauties of the Song is that the bridegroom saw something of himself in her, and she saw herself in him. What could have been better than to hear him say, *"O fairest among women"*? How well she knew how he looked upon her and saw her loveliness, and then drew comparisons with himself.

- They had mutual fairness (1:15 ; and 16 RV);
- They had dove-like eyes (1:15; 5:12);
- They were similarly distinguished (5:10; 6:4);
- There was a glory in their lips (4:3, 11; 5:13);
- They were fragrant in character (1:12; 4:11; 7:8; 1:3).

Firstly, there was a beauty in her that reflected his brightness, and they could see it in each other. How deeply challenging this is, for no matter how long we have journeyed with the Saviour, learning of Him and absorbing Him can be two very different things. Only when He moves us do they become the same, but have we been sufficiently moved? Until then, every act of unfairness or injustice, every unpleasant thought, word or deed, betrays how little we resemble the One whom God sent as *"the brightness of His glory."*[17]

Secondly, there was purity in her. Apart from telling her that she had *"dove's eyes,"* three times over he calls her *"My dove,"*[18] so the tenderness of her eyes was matched by the gentleness of her nature. It is also well known that doves have very attentive, undistracted vision, which focus on one thing, and that they are constantly stabilising and sharpening their focus as they walk. Unlike the dove, the first-mentioned bird in Scripture is the raven whose habit is so different. Having been sent out by Noah from the ark, its unsettled flight continued and *"kept going to and fro until the waters had dried up from the earth."*[19] By contrast, the dove twice showed its homing instinct: firstly, after finding no rest, which didn't enter the raven's mind, and then with the evidence of safety in her mouth. Perhaps it was from this imagery that David thought of his own struggles and said, *"Oh, that I had wings like a dove! I would fly away and be at rest ... I would hasten my escape from the windy storm and tempest."*[20]

The raven is named *"as an abomination among the birds"* in Leviticus 11:13,15 and as unclean in Deuteronomy 14:14, while the dove was not only clean, but accepted as an offering on God's altar.[21] In keeping with these lovely features, God also deemed two doves to be a suitable offering from Joseph and Mary at the time of purification following the birth of the Lord Jesus.[22] As we know, God also used the dove as symbol of the Holy Spirit's descent on Jesus at His baptism,[23] so altogether the dove has been given a very special place in His Word, not only befitting of the bride and bridegroom's nature, but of the divine nature too.

Winter is past

It was as if the seasons changed at the sound of his voice, and there was real need for a change in her condition: from shared thoughts in chapter 1 to shared voices in chapter 2. Thoughts and memories may survive at a distance, but it takes closeness to welcome the value of a voice. Evidently, it had been missing, and the beloved saw these times like unwanted wintry conditions of darkness, cold, and rain. Having shared her thoughts, it is time for him to share his, and in response to her cry, *"Let him,"* he didn't offer a corresponding, 'Let her,' but gave his double appeal, *"Let me ... Let me."* The one whose *"eyes are like doves"* wanted to see his *"dove,"* but he also wanted to hear her voice. He could see flowers were blossoming and hear *"the voice of the turtledove,"* but her voice was unheard. Would springtime's revival cause their friendship to blossom, and let the sound of her voice be heard? In the blast of wintry conditions, he thought of his dove *"in the cleft of the rock, in the secret places of the cliff."*[24] In his knowledge of birdlife,[25] he knew the dove's habitat as another place of shadow, a safe and sheltered place in the recesses of the rocks.

Time after time, God applied such imagery to His people, partly through David, *"You shall hide them in the secret place of Your presence,"*[26] and *"You are my hiding place; You shall preserve me from trouble."*[27] He also reassured them through Isaiah of a great day that's coming when *"A man will be as a hiding place from the wind, and a cover from the tempest; as rivers of water in a dry place, as the shadow of a great rock in a weary land."*[28] What a great day when Israel, at last, turns to Christ for, because of Him, *"The eyes of those who see will not be dim, and the ears of those who hear will listen."*[29] They will turn to Him as their King, and as their Beloved. It will be as if He says, "Let Me, let Me," and they will! Their eye will be single, like the focus of the dove, they will hear the voice of their Redeemer-Messiah saying, *"This is My people;"* and, like turtledoves returning after a long winter, He will hear each one of them saying, *"The LORD is my God."*[30] What a Man! And we are hidden in Him.[31]

Until ... the shadows flee away

Sometimes there are shadows in our lives that are self-inflicted. The bride had them. They were cast over her friendship because of her 'see you later' attitude towards him. It was as if she had said, 'Don't call me, I'll call you.' It seems significant that *"the shadows"* of verse 17 follow *"the foxes"* in verse 15. How often our failings, even petty failings - *"the little foxes"* - spoil our life with the Lord, and cast shadows. The problem with little foxes is that they grow and end up producing more. Her beloved offered to help her get rid of them. *"Catch us"* shows that the Lord will not do this for us, but He will do it with us. Shadows of doubt, departure and disobedience can build up *"mountains of Bether"* – mountains of separation and division. How much we need our Beloved's help, if our shadows are to flee away! But how long is our *"until"*?

After some lambs had been killed one year, we tracked foxes back to their lair on a nearby farm. As we stood around it, a sharp-eyed old shepherd came over the hillside and, reaching the lair, immediately bent down to pick up the remains of a lamb's foot. He was a vivid reminder of the shepherd in Amos 3:12 *"who takes from the mouth of a lion two legs or a piece of an ear,"* as proof that he did all he could to rescue, but came home only with the evidence of a casualty.

Oh for *"a morning without clouds"*![32] Life has so many of them, when circumstances, events, illness and bereavement cast their gloomy veil. Unlike the shadows of chapters 1:8 and 2:3, where the shade is for comfort, the shadows in chapters 2:17 and 4:6 are the result of calamity. Even though we might say, *"My days are like a shadow that lengthens,"*[33] or *"Our days on earth are as a shadow,"*[34] we seek the LORD, since *"He turns the shadow of death into morning."*[35]

He had His own mountain of Bether, where He knew the horrors of separation and division as He made the great atonement. His cross was the place of which He could have said, *"I will go my way to the mountain of myrrh and to the hill of frankincense."*[36] Myrrh is associated with His deep suffering, and it was a steep *"mountain"* for Him to ascend.[37] The frankincense refers to the fragrance that ascended to God from Him as the accepted Sacrifice[38] and, from this aspect of His offering, Calvary was a *"hill"* that He went up in the full joy of what it would accomplish. [39] Golgotha was a mountain and a hill for Him, and from its height He calls us to – *"Look from the top."*-[40]

From there, we have a better vantage point from which to view our shadows. We can look upward to heaven as well as downward on our hurts. By prayer, we can experience His promise that, *"those who wait on the LORD ... shall mount up with wings like eagles."*[41] Then we will see our clouds from the upper side, in the light of the sun. In the light of His presence, we can view our shadows from above instead of underneath. Like Him, we can see the frankincense in our cross and not only the myrrh!

THE BANYAN TREE
To sit beneath the banyan tree
With numerous boughs outspreading,
And sense its dark philosophy ,
Is darkness well worth dreading.
A pantheistic view of God
Depicted in its tendrils
Obscures the nature of the One
Who warns against such perils.

A multiplicity of gods

Are bound within this ancient shrine;
Theirs is a different mind from God,
Which makes no difference to mine.
Though myriad stems uphold the tree,
And myriad gods presented be,
The emptiness that fills the place
Cries out to know the God of grace.

In different climes, in different times,
A bride with her beloved reclines, (Song 2:3)
And views him as an apple tree –
No large and spreading Banyan he!
As tree, it is less visible;
Its fruit, much more accessible,
The one true God, their safe retreat, (Is.46:9)
And Israel bows down at His feet.

So, then, shall we who love the Lord
And know the comfort of His Word,
Find in the Man of Calvary,
Who bore the shame and agony,
An ever-perfect resting place
Of goodness, mercy, and of grace,
That none can ever claim to see
Beneath the Godless Banyan tree.
[Written after visiting The Theosophical Society in
Adyar, Madras South India with Guy Jarvie in 1977]

4

GLORY

> *"I am the rose of Sharon,*
> *And the lily of the valleys.*
> *Like a lily among thorns,*
> *So is my love among the daughters.*
> *My beloved has gone to his garden,*
> *To the beds of spices,*
> *To feed his flock in the gardens,*
> *And to gather lilies."*
> (Song of Songs 2:1, 2; 6:2)

* * *

I am ... the lily of the valleys. Like a lily among thorns.

Some have taken the lily of the valleys to refer to the Lord Jesus Christ Himself, perhaps on the basis of a hymn that says so, but most commentators believe this to be the bride's view of herself. Having already described herself as *"dark, but lovely,"* she now compares herself to a rose and a lily. But it would appear that she is speaking about herself in comparison to other roses of the plain and to other lilies of the valleys. Speaking in a comparative way didn't suit her beloved, and he chose to adopt a contrast by seeing her as *"a lily among thorns."* She thought of herself among other lilies that resembled her; he thought of her as exclusively beautiful among thorns. In other words, she stood out as unique among Eden's curse; set apart as Israel was to God, and as the bride of Christ will be to Him. As sinners, we share its curse; as believers, we share His glory. On His way to, and at, Calvary, though wearing the reminder of the curse, He was crowned with thorns by the outsiders of the garden, yet crowned with glory and honour by the One who had been within.

It takes the Man of Calvary to bring Old Testament truth and type into the reality of inspired harmony, and He proved this when He asked His disciple to *"Consider the lilies of the field, how they grow, they neither toil nor spin; and yet I say to you that even Solomon in all his glory was not arrayed like one of these."*[6] How beautifully He elevated the imagery of the Song! Yes, He sees *"the lilies of the field,"* but had He not also seen *"the lily of the valleys"* and watched her growth while, at the same time, watching the see-sawing changes in the experience of God's people? In all these, the two pillars of Solomon's temple stood unchanged, not least their tops, which *"were in the shape of lilies."* While they stood, they demonstrated the meaning of their names, Jachin and Boaz, "He shall establish" and "In it is strength."[7] They also announce the thought that temple testimony was crowned with glory, as represented in the lilies. The same portion goes on to describe the huge laver, the brim of which was like a flowering lily to depict the glory of His Word. The remarkable thing is, it's His Word that tells us about His glory: both the incommunicable and the communicable. For example:

*In creation

As Psalms 8 and 19 open on the theme of creation, they both lift our thoughts to the transcendent glory of God. Irrespective of their particular focus, be it in His creative handiwork and finger work, in natural laws that govern the heavens or spiritual laws that govern man, all of these are intended to raise our sights to His glory. The wonders of the heavens take us even higher, to dwell on the One who has *"set His glory above"* them. Likewise, His brilliance in the skies presents a unique display of orbital order that can fascinate the most enquiring mind. But there's more to it than that. While it is worthy of closest investigation, the declaration that is being made is worthy of our fullest attention for *"the heavens declare the glory of God."*

Understandably, people of every nation can be absorbed and intrigued by what they are seeing, but we ought also to be engrossed by what we should be hearing. *"There is no speech nor language where their voice is not heard. Their line has gone out through all the earth, and their words to the end of the world."*[8] The truth is, God is speaking as well as showing, but are we as interested in hearing as we are in seeing? Visiting a planetarium will inevitably leave us spellbound. The formation of constellations declare a Former; the seemingly endless arrangement of galaxies declare an infinite Arranger; and the glory that is within them points us higher to the glory that is above them: God!

He presently announces the declaration of His glory in His creation, and has been doing it all along: *"For since the creation of the world His invisible attributes are clearly seen, being understood by the things that are made, even His eternal power and Godhead, so that they are without excuse."*[9] He will do it again in the future:

"The wilderness and the wasteland shall be glad for them,
And the desert shall rejoice and blossom as the rose;
It shall blossom abundantly and rejoice,
Even with joy and singing.
The glory of Lebanon shall be given to it,
The excellence of Carmel and Sharon.
They shall see the glory of the LORD,
The excellency of our God."[10]

Every valley shall be exalted
And every mountain and hill brought low;
The crooked places shall be made straight
And the rough places smooth;
The glory of the LORD shall be revealed,
And all flesh shall see it together;
For the mouth of the LORD has spoken."[11]

*In the church in the wilderness

There were times in the Shulamite's relationship with Solomon that "Ichabod" could have been written over it for it seems that "The glory had departed." There's no mention of the word "glory" in the Song, even when beauty, majesty and dignity were evident, and it's all very reminiscent of the reaction shown by Phinehas' wife when she called her newborn son Ichabod and said, *"The glory has departed from Israel, because the ark of God had been captured."*[12] Its former home had been in the Most Holy Place of the tabernacle and temple. Of the first, God said, *"The tabernacle shall be sanctified by My glory,"*[13] and He also said of the temple, *"The glory of the LORD filled the house of the LORD."*[14] This was the declaration of God's glory in His house, yet His people whom He had *"formed"*[15] for Himself didn't always serve Him in ways that echoed

37

the declaration of His glory in creation.

The temple should have been the place where everything was set apart in holiness to God and from all else, but, in Haggai's day, some were concerned about the sense of His glory. Their plight could be summed up as follows:

- **RECOLLECTION OF FORMER GLORY** - "Who is left among you who saw this temple in its former glory?" (2:3);
- **EVALUATION OF PRESENT GLORY** - "And how do you see it now? In comparison with it, is this not in your eyes as nothing?" (2:3);
- **ANTICIPATION OF FUTURE GLORY** - "The glory of this latter temple shall be greater than the former" (2:9).

The bridal language of the song, and later of Hosea, tends to mirror Israel's inglorious relationship with God, yet, just as she enjoyed a glorious end with her beloved, so also will Israel. Along with the promise of greater glory, the God of glory gave this added assurance, *"And in this place I will give peace."* Peace? Even though their names, Sh^{e}lomoh and Shulammith, both mean "peaceful," it's another of the missing words in the Song, until we come to chapter 8:10. It's there Solomon proves the truth of his own words in Ecclesiastes 7:8, *"The end of a thing is better than its beginning."* As the end of the Song approaches, his bride makes this marvellous claim, *"Then I became in his eyes as one who found peace."* So it will be, at last, for those who began their journey as *"the church in the wilderness."*[16] They will come, just as the bride is seen, *"Coming up from the wilderness, leaning upon her beloved.*[17] *"A greater than Solomon* [will be] *here,"* and, leaning on Him, she will say, *"And this man shall be our peace."*[18] Hosea also takes up this triumphant theme, as he anticipates the day when God will heal His people's backsliding and love them freely. He *"will be like the dew to Israel; he shall grow like the lily.*"[19] God will see His glory in them, and be able to call them, *"Israel My glory,"*[20] because the Lord also made peace for them through the blood of His cross.

In days of great need God had spoken through prophets, such as Jeremiah and Haggai: *"Amend your ways"*[21] and *"Consider your ways!"*[22] It was as if the voice of the Beloved was knocking, but Israel's neglect caused the enemy to destroy the pillars, Jachin and Boaz, and their lily work. It was only then they discovered the pillars were hollow[23], something they should never have known. Alas, it was a voice that the people were the same! As the people, so the pillars: God showed that His glory no longer remains when the foundations and strength have gone! How well we need to remember that shallowness and hollowness can be next-door neighbours! Falling standards of holiness, of prayerfulness, or steadfastness in the Word will affect the demonstration of His glory, and God is not unconditionally tied to us when this happens.

*In Christ

In introducing the Son of God from heaven, John wrote, *"In the beginning was the Word, and the Word was with God, and the Word was God. He was in the beginning with God. All things were made through Him, and without Him nothing was made that was made."* He is the One through whom the glory of God is still being "declared" in the heavens, but He also is the One in whom we see the glory that is *"above the heavens!"* He is not only above them, He is before them for He already was in the beginning when He brought them into existence. In contrast to being the One through whom God has "declared" His glory in creation, but not all of it, the Son does show all of it, for *"He has declared Him."*[24]

As John viewed Him, he said, *"we beheld His glory,"*[25] and on a day-today basis, this was true as they walked and talked with a sinless Man. They saw the glory of His perfect body and holy nature. They also saw it in His miracles, beginning at the marriage in Cana where He *"manifested His glory."*[26] Like water drawn from the lily-brimmed laver, with a few words He showed that His lips are like lilies. *"Fill the waterpots with water. Draw some out now, and take it to the master of the feast."*[27] Being filled to the brim, these servants could see that it was water, and they knew very well that water from these vessels was for hand-washing, not for drinking. Even so, they drew, and as it was drawn it changed to wine. They knew it had not been sourced from an Israeli vineyard, that no clusters had been harvested and trampled in a winepress, so drawing was an act of faith. It was as if they were given an object lesson to show that faith in the Son of God turns the Word of God into a work of God, and the Word of the Lord into the joy of the Lord. They knew that He was the source and, coming from Him, as He would reveal later, it was from the Vine, not the vineyard!

Through six filled waterpots He manifested His glory, but these were the measure of His blessing, not the measure of His glory! The voice of the true Beloved was knocking, but was there any response from the bride and groom, or guests? All we know is, that *"His disciples believed in Him,"* having just witnessed a manifestation of the glory of God. However, the greater glory that He left when He *"emptied Himself"*[28] was veiled in His humanity, except when *"He was transfigured before them. His face shone like the sun, and His clothes became white as the light."*[29] This was a unique glimpse of what we will see *"when His glory is revealed.*[30] Not until then shall we see the full declaration of God's glory in His Son, and His infinite splendour as the *"brightness of His glory."*[31]

*In His church

God's pleasure in His Son is expressly presented in Isaiah 53:10 in association with the grief of making His soul an offering for sin, and the verse concludes with that same pleasure prospering through His nail-pierced hand, because *"He shall see His seed."* This is the same pleasure that God announced in Matthew 17:5 in association with His Son's glory. How fitting it was that God's announcement should come after His Son's announcement in chapter 16:18 and 21, *"on this rock I will build My church"* and *"that He must go to Jerusalem, and suffer ... and be killed, and be raised on the third day."* As Peter looked back on the majesty of his Saviour *"on the holy mountain,"* he gave the reason for it: *"For He received from God the Father honor and glory when such a voice came to Him from the Excellent Glory: "This is My beloved Son, in whom I am well pleased.""*[32]

It was with the same pleasure that God the Father, the Excellent Glory, crowned Him with glory and honour *"for the suffering of death."*[33] Even though the cross held such horror for Him, with all this divine pleasure in mind, He went out bearing His cross *"for the joy that was set before Him."*[34] He had received glory *from* God knowing that He would give glory *to* God by glorifying Him by finishing the work He had given Him to do.[35]

We also rejoice that the outcome of His finished work causes us to say with Paul in Ephesians 3:21, *"To Him be glory in* [Gr. *en]* *the church by* [Gr. *en:* in] *Christ Jesus to all generations, forever and ever. Amen."* God will have eternal glory *in* the church and *in* His Son. How wonderful, He will be glorified in Christ and in all those who are in Christ! The Builder and the church will give Him glory; the Head and the members will give Him glory, and the Bridegroom and the bride will give Him glory.

By faith we see the glory
Of which Thou dost assure us,
The world despise
For that high prize
Which Thou hast set before us.
We wait with expectation
The happy consummation
Of that blest promise given,
To meet our Lord
By all adored,
And swell the praise of heaven.
(Charles Wesley)

My beloved has gone down ... to gather lilies.

What a lovely occupation for the beloved! He was gathering lilies that resembled him, and it depicts the declaration of the Lord's glory in His own. He wants to share His glory with us and to gather it from us. The Christian should be able to say, like David, *"In God is my salvation and my glory."*[36] He began by gathering those He calls to eternal life through *"the gospel of the glory of Christ,"*[37] and He will end, either by calling us through death or at the return of our Lord Jesus Christ. How comforting it is to borrow the imagery of the Song when loved ones are called home to glory, and say, "My Beloved has gone down into His garden to gather lilies." He has opened our eyes to what we have in Christ, but He also wants us to see what Christ has in us: *"the eyes of your understanding being enlightened; that you may know what is the hope of His calling, what are the riches of the glory of His inheritance in the saints, and what is the exceeding greatness of His power toward us who believe."*[38] This is far beyond the glory of His finger-work and handiwork. It's the glory of His cross-work! Through His death and resurrection, the voice of our

Beloved is still calling us to show that we are vessels of mercy that He has prepared beforehand for glory.[39]

- "That you may be filled with the knowledge of His will in all wisdom and spiritual understanding" (Col.1:9) - **THE GLORY OF OUR SUBMISSION**;
- "That you may walk worthy of the Lord, fully pleasing Him" (Col.1:10) - **THE GLORY OF OUR DIRECTION**;
- "being fruitful in every good work" (Col.1:10) - **THE GLORY OF OUR PRODUCTION**;
- "and increasing in the knowledge of God" (Col.1:10) - **THE GLORY OF OUR INSTRUCTION**;
- "Strengthened with all might, according to His glorious power" (Col.1:11) - **THE GLORY OF OUR CONDITION**.

What lofty language! Each of us is called to be enabled with His miraculous power, according to the dignified, honourable vigour of His glory. And there ought to be a reflection of His glory in each of us as we endeavour to fulfil 2 Corinthians 3:18 – *"But we all, with unveiled face, beholding as in a mirror the glory of the Lord, are being transformed into the same image from glory to glory, just as by the Spirit of the Lord."* What a wonderful possibility! The highest of all desires! But how shall we achieve it, unless we learn to cry, *"Please, show me Your glory."*[40]

CHRIST, THE TRANSFORMING LIGHT
Christ, The Transforming Light,
Touches this heart of mine,
Piercing the darkest night,
Making His glory shine.

Oh, to reflect His grace,
Causing the world to see
Love that will glow, till others shall know
Jesus, revealed in me.

Here, Lord, I bring my heart,
My love, my strength, my will,
Cleanse me in every part,
With all Thy Spirit fill.

Life is no longer mine,
I yield it all to Thee;
Fill me, that I may shine,
Until Thy face I see.

Triumphant peace is mine,
Now Jesus reigns with-in;
He giveth joy divine,
And vict'ry over sin.
(Gipsy Smith)

5

WALLS

"The voice of my beloved! Behold, he comes
Leaping upon the mountains, skipping upon the hills.
My beloved is like a gazelle or a young stag.
Behold, he stands behind our wall;
He is looking through the windows,
Gazing through the lattice.
My beloved spoke, and said to me:
Rise up, my love, my fair one, and come away.
I am a wall,
And my breasts like towers;
Then I became in his eyes as one who found peace."
(Song of Songs 2:8-10; 8:10)

* * *

If only our walk with the Lord was always consistent! In the course of this Song there are great changes in the bride's attitudes and actions. This is very noticeable when her *"I am"* in chapter 1:5 is contrasted with her final *"I am"* in chapter 8:10. Along the way, during

45

the eight chapters, we will discover a series of walls, barriers that show the kind of hindrances that can interfere with our own love-bond with Christ our Beloved.

It's both interesting and significant in Romans 12 to notice how Paul began outlining how a Christian should present his or her body as a living sacrifice, which is our *logikēn latreian*, our logical, reasonable service or our spiritual worship. Before entering into what we might do as gifted members of the *"one body in Christ,"* he deals with how we might think. This isn't simply important; it's imperative. In following the Christ of the lowly mind, it's essential that we allow the Spirit of God to produce lowliness of mind in us. To be effective for the Lord in our doing, we must become like Him in our thinking. This was paramount to the apostle, and it's not accidental that, when he began to speak to the Philippians about encouragement, comfort and unity, he urged them:

> *"Let nothing be done through selfish ambition or conceit, but in lowliness of mind let each esteem others better than himself. Let each of you look out not only for his own interests, but also for the interests of others. Let this mind be in you which was also in Christ Jesus."*[1]

Once again, it begins in the mind with how we think! Not surprisingly, it's the first barrier we find in the Song.

A PSYCHOLOGICAL WALL – "I am dark"

Strange as it may seem, the first obstacle in the Song follows her vow in verse 4. She began with a real expression of joy from which came her vow, and this shows how love for, and joy in, the Lord will cause us to make further pledges. She seemed to be overflowing, and then came the triple promise: *"we will ... we will ... we will,"* but suddenly, and unexpectedly, a wall is built in verse 5. As Christians, we can be encouraged by this for sometimes it's the fear of relapse that keeps us back from making a vow of commitment at all. The Lord knows that we will have our down times, but He still wants a personal pledge from each of us.

Lack of self-esteem, self-doubt, an under-estimation of herself, an inferiority complex, formed her first hurdle. At the front of her mind was her admission of what she felt about herself: *"I am dark."* It was an admission of all that she was naturally. *"Dark"* describes what she was; *"lovely"* tells us that she was accepted as she was. It's a word that means 'suitable' or 'beautiful.' The tents and the curtains may have been dark, but she knew they were suitable. It may have been that the tents were dark and the curtains were lovely, but it was what they were to their owners that mattered. If only she had shifted the emphasis by saying, *"I am lovely, but dark"*! She was important to her bridegroom, and we are to ours. We have been *"accepted in the Beloved."*[2] Two things emerge: she had to learn how valuable he was, and she had to learn how valuable she was, not to herself, but to him.

In Christian growth, we also have to learn how valuable Christ is to us and how valuable we are to Him. A sense of unworthiness should never become a barrier to spiritual progress or usefulness. By the adversary's subtlety it can become inverted pride. For example, we could say "I'm not good enough, strong enough or useful enough," but will we ever reach the stage when we would say, "Lord, I'm good enough, strong enough and useful enough"? How much better it is, if we see ourselves in 1 Corinthians 1:26-29 as foolish, weak, base, despised and nothing! The Lord can do something with our justifiable sense of inadequacy, but He can do nothing with a superiority complex other than to humble it.

He chose us to bless us, to enrich, and to use us. We are valuable to Him!

In chapter 1:9, the bridegroom demolished her wall in a very gracious way with his premeditated estimation of her worth. How patiently he did it: *"O my love."* There was no sense of frustration or exasperation. Speaking to her about the steeds of Pharaoh's chariots was his way of reassuring her. Really, he was saying, *"They are valuable, elegant and courageous – and so are you!"* He also reminded her that she was *"lovely"*: in chapter 1:10, her cheeks; in chapter 2:14, her face; in chapter 4:3, her mouth; and in chapter 6:4, in her entirety. How carefully he dismantled her psychological wall.

We ought to let the Lord do this for us whenever we feel down about our own inadequacy. He will encourage us by reminding us of the price He paid for us, of the standing we have in Him, and the courage we have through Him.

A PHYSICAL WALL – "Behind our wall"

Another barrier was her lack of self-motivation and a tendency to self-pity. The bridegroom had followed up her vow, undoubtedly expecting a positive response. Strangely, there was none. She had promised, *"We will run,"* yet she was not even prepared to crawl. Inertia had taken over, and a total lack of effort! Her reaction was so selfish and showed no appreciation of all the effort and activity he had shown toward her:

- In verse 8 – speaking … leaping … skipping;
- In verse 9 – standing … looking … gazing;
- In verse 10 – appealing.

By her sluggish reaction she seemed to say, "You could have saved yourself the trouble." His reassuring voice of chapter 1 now has no impact, and all the energy he expended was to no avail. She was playing hard-to-get, and brought him to a standstill. Notice what she said: *"He stands behind our wall."* Why implicate him? It was her wall! But isn't it so natural to share the blame! Sometimes, when Christians are going through a difficult patch, they say, "Christianity doesn't work. God doesn't speak to us. The Lord doesn't seem real." It's our way of blaming Him for *"our wall."* The bridegroom's activity reminds us of the Lord's willingness to make Himself available and His desire to speak. The church in Laodicea brought Him to a standstill in Revelation 3:20, and so can we. But He *"will wait that He may be gracious to you."*[3]

As the bridegroom waited, he was *"looking through the windows."* going round the house from room to room, like the Lord examining the compartments of our lives and homes. She could see him move from one window to another. Each window was a new opportunity for a fresh vision of her beloved, a new appeal. He knew she was there and tried his best to make an impact on her by standing in different places where he could be seen. But each window was a different viewpoint for him, too! Are there windows in your life that give opportunities for seeing Christ, and for Him to see you? We all have rooms in our lives, like different compartments. Have you drawn the blinds in some, shutting yourself in and Him out, trying to keep the contents secret? Even so, He is still interested in you. And still waiting!

Then he spent time *"gazing through the lattice."* The word *"gazing"* can be translated as "showing, glancing, glittering, or blossoming" and this illustrates how he stood there long enough to glitter and blossom before her eyes and heart. Apparently she didn't think about the disappointment she was causing him. Isn't that just like us? We get so taken up with how we feel that we don't stop to think about how He feels or the hurt He suffers. There are times when He says to us, *"Rise up, my love, my fair one, and come away."* It's as if He is saying, "I know you are down, but don't stay down. You are distant, but don't remain at a distance. I have come that we might be together." He knows and cares about our lethargy, depression, and so on. He knows it doesn't always take major things to knock us off course, yet He still stands and waits, as if to say, *"I will heal their backsliding, I will love them freely."*[4] Even when darkness surrounds us, like the bride in chapter 3:1, He waits to hear us saying, *"The night also is Yours."*[5]

Building a personal relationship demands the demolition of such barriers for they are real, like all physical walls. Her beloved took care of the wall in chapter 1, but the wall in chapter 2 she would have to remove herself. We have such walls:

- Lack of self-motivation;
- A closed home;
- Habits and hobbies;
- Seeking help from the wrong people: secular counsellors who don't use the Word or through relationships with non-Christians.

Any of these can build a wall around the conscience. Have you ever asked Him to demolish these kinds of walls for you?

At the end of chapter 1, we thought about her awareness of his protection affecting her senses. Now he appeals to her hearing by speaking and knocking, and later to her sense of touch by reaching in his hand.[6] In our own relationship with the Saviour our spiritual senses need to be moved by the hearing of faith,[7] by seeing our calling,[8] and, like Noah, moved with godly fear.[9]

If we put chapter 3:1 and 5:2,3 together, it is evident that the bride preferred her bed to her beloved, being under the sheet to being under the shadow, her blanket to his banner. Self-will had taken over, and self-motivation had gone. Bed can be a place for thoughtful meditation and resolve as Psalm 63:6-8 shows: *"When I remember You on my bed, I meditate on You in the night watches. Because You have been my help, therefore in the shadow of Your wings I will rejoice. My soul follows close behind You; Your right hand upholds me."* Sadly, it can be the indication of idleness and lack of enthusiasm. Three God-given exercises will keep us from laziness:

- **READING**: This is one channel through which He can speak with us on a daily basis;
- **PRAYER**: This allows us to speak with Him on a daily basis;
- **COMMUNION**: This will mean knowing His presence with us, directing our day, helping us through. Just being aware that He is there.[10]

In chapter 5:2, she admitted to being asleep and to hearing *"the voice of my beloved! He knocks."* The Hebrew word for *"knocks"* is translated in Genesis 33:13 as *"overdrive"* (RV). Maybe we don't like the idea of being put into overdrive, but God calls for it in Amos 6:1, by saying, *"Woe to you who are at ease in Zion."* He also reminds us again, in Ephesians 5:14, *"Awake, you who sleep, arise from the dead, and Christ will give you light."*

The bridegroom wanted action, she didn't. She searched for him in bed and in the streets: two unlikely places for him! What did he think about her reluctance and about her having to ask strangers for directions? When we seek the Lord we have to seek Him in the right way and in the right place. Making excuses is a sure sign of relapse and wrong condition. Comforts were a wall to her. Putting on a coat was too big an effort, and dirtying the feet she had washed didn't appeal to her either. This was the wall of self-satisfaction and self-indulgence. As a nation, Israel had these weaknesses, but she learned that her feet were defiled when she walked away from the Lord toward idolatry, not when she returned. What a lesson: it's the direction that defiles not the surface! *"Robe"* refers to Israel's testimony and *"feet"* refers to Israel's walk. One thing we need to learn is this, we don't ever get defiled or soil our feet by walking with Christ.

Her heart became agitated – *"yearned for him"* – when she saw his hand, but the hands that were like *"rings of gold"* (RV) were left empty. Instead of walking hand-in-hand with him, she went around the city calling for him. What a poor advertisement she was as she went searching and shouting! Her behaviour exposed her to maltreatment, misinterpretation and mockery. Watchmen looked for vagrants, troublemakers and harlots, so it wasn't surprising that she was taken for one and treated as one.

It's very noticeable that it was when she tried to get back to her beloved that all this happened. This is when the world will ill-treat and abuse the Christian. There is no attack on the silent believer or on the secret disciple. They took away her *"veil"* (5:7) - her bridegroom knew what was behind it. It was like a wall behind which lay a mind and features that were reserved for him. Now they became public knowledge. Reserved love has reserved thoughts! Our minds ought to be reserved for Christ, though the world will try to rob us of what is enclosed for Him. It will never direct us to Him, wishing rather to make us feel cheap, cheated, distracted and disgraced. The stirring of her heart brought the stirring of her feet. Signs of life, at last! The Lord wants to see them now – in you. What will it take? Something you read for yourself? Something you hear from someone else? He wants your company, whatever it takes!

He may use what you are reading from his Word or He may use others. The secret still is, "Let Him"!

> Lord, when I'm weary with toiling,
> And burdensome seem Your commands,
> If my load should lead to complaining,
> Lord, show me Your hands –
> Your nail-pierced hands, Your cross-torn hands,
> My Saviour, show me Your hands.
> (Amy Carmichael)

OTHER WALLS

In the language of The Song, the garden in chapter 4:12, 16 etc. was a walled place; so too were the villages and the vineyards. Each was enclosed for their pleasure and, when at last, she also brought pleasure to her beloved, she was able to be one. God's purpose is still the same for women He moves, *"Therefore we also pray always for you that our God would count you worthy of this calling, and fulfill all the good pleasure of His goodness and the work of faith with power."*[11]

"I am a wall"

Final triumph! Ultimate enjoyment! She became so at one with her beloved that she demonstrates the value of a wall: a woman with total separation, total affection, and total protection. In each, she was totally upright, strong, well grounded and no pushover! Spiritual stability is always the mark of a spiritual man or woman, and God has His own way of moving them, so that in every other way they become immoveable. *"Therefore, my beloved brethren, be steadfast, immovable, always abounding in the work of the Lord, knowing that your labour is not in vain in the Lord.*"[12] Is this what you want to be for Him? If so, Jesus says to you, *"Take up [your] cross daily, and follow Me."*[13] Would you like to be *"a wall"*? If so, *"Take up the whole armour of God, that you may be able to withstand in the evil day, and having done all, to stand."*[14]

When all the bride's earlier walls had been demolished, only then could she be one herself. And so it will be with us, too, when we find ourselves resting at last, not in the self-sufficient but in the All-sufficient!

TOMORROW

Lord, what am I, that, with unceasing care,
Thou didst seek after me, that Thou didst wait,
Wet with unhealthy dews before my gate,
And pass the gloomy nights of winter there?
O strange delusion – that I did not greet
Thy blest approach, and O, to Heaven how lost,
If my ingratitude's unkindly frost
Has chilled the bleeding wounds upon Thy feet.
How oft my guardian angel gently cried,
"Soul, from thy casement look, and thou shalt see
How He persists to knock and wait for thee!"
And, O! how often to that voice of sorrow,
"Tomorrow we will open," I replied,
And when the morrow came I answered still, "Tomorrow."
(Henry Wadsworth Longfellow)

6

HIS DESCRIPTION OF HER

"Behold, you are fair, my love! Behold, you are fair!
You have dove's eyes behind your veil.
Your hair is like a flock of goats, going down from Mount Gilead.
Your teeth are like a flock of shorn sheep
Which have come up from the washing,
Every one of which bears twins,
And none is barren among them.
Your lips are like a strand of scarlet, and your mouth is lovely.
Your temples behind your veil are like a piece of pomegranate.
Your neck is like the tower of David, built for an armory,
On which hang a thousand bucklers, all shields of mighty men.
Your two breasts are like two fawns,
Twins of a gazelle, which feed among the lilies."
(Song of Songs 4:1-5)

* * *

T wo complementary things are essential in any couple's love bond: how he sees her, and how she sees him. They can speak generally of each other, but they are equally ready to speak particularly and intimately. The Song's imagery is typically eastern, and the western mind will find it difficult to relate to it, except for the underlying purpose that what they saw in each other has direct bearing on how God viewed His people, Israel, and how the Lord Jesus Christ views his church. When Solomon, the beloved in the Song, wrote his Proverbs, certain guideline thoughts were at the forefront of his mind, and they are amply expressed in chapter 2:10 and 11. *"When wisdom enters your heart, and knowledge is pleasant to your soul, discretion will preserve you; understanding will keep you."* He also makes it clear right from the beginning, in chapter 9:10, that *"The fear of the LORD is the beginning of wisdom."* By this, he means that reverence for God is "the principal thing"; and then, in chapter 4:7, he states that *"Wisdom is the principal thing; therefore get wisdom. And in all your getting, get understanding."*

Following this lead, we would endeavour to let due reverence for God bring wisdom to our hearts and souls, so that *"The Spirit of wisdom and understanding"*[1] will help us properly to interpret and apply this portion of God's Word. Our only aim is to see what He wants us to see, and to share in its pleasantness, therefore we align ourselves with Paul's prayer in Ephesians 1:17, *"that the God of our Lord Jesus Christ, the Father of glory, may give to you the spirit of wisdom and revelation in the knowledge of Him."* With this in mind, we keep Solomon's four stages before us.

- The need for **wisdom**: that only God can give;
- The need for **knowledge**: to know only what He wants us to know;
- The need for **discretion**: to think as we ought to think;
- The need for **understanding**: not fanciful thoughts, but God-given

56

intelligence.

Behold, you are fair

He had already voiced this double endearment in chapter 1:15 and her intervening tardiness didn't make him change his mind or keep him from repeating it. How reassuring it must have been to hear him say that he found her to be entirely beautiful, and that nothing dimmed her brightness to him! Her own self-deprecating comments about herself made no difference to him: it wasn't her blackness that impressed him, but her brightness. And so it was with Israel, and is with us.

Much more than tardiness blighted the walk of God's people, yet He assured them, *"Yes, I have loved you with an everlasting love; therefore with lovingkindness I have drawn you."*[2] Oh, it wasn't that He thought little of their waywardness; it was just that He thought more of winning them back. Even while Hosea fulfilled his heart-breaking ministry, God cried, *"How can I give you up, Ephraim? How can I hand you over, Israel?"*[3] In the closing stage of His appeal, He gave His promise, *"I will heal their backsliding, I will love them freely, for My anger has turned away from him."*[4]

Yes, there will be times when the Lord is just as disappointed in us, and maybe there are times when you are tempted to think He no longer has anything to say to you or anything for you to do for Him. No, He will not give you up or hand you over. It didn't happen under Law, and it won't happen under grace! We never will be failure-less. He knows this, more than we know it ourselves, and He waits for us to return. Is our Bridegroom not more able than the Shulamite's to show that our challenges don't make Him change His mind? Remember, a greater than Solomon is here, and He is far more able to remind those who belong to Him, *"Behold you are fair, My love! Behold, you are fair!"*

Our bridal bond with Christ is beautifully depicted in Psalm 45 where the bride is told in verse 11, *"So the King will greatly desire your beauty,"* and, in response, we can have no greater desire than *"To behold the beauty of the LORD."*[5]

His oath, His covenant, His blood,
Support me in the whelming flood;
When all around my soul gives way,
He then is all my hope and stay.

When He shall come with trumpet sound,
Oh, may I then in Him be found;
In Him, my righteousness, alone,
Faultless to stand before the throne.
(Edward Mote)

You have dove's eyes – 4:1; 7:4

This is how verse 1 appears in the New King James Version. The King James Version says, "doves' eyes", and some others translate it as "eyes are doves." Solomon actually referred to doves in the plural, to show that the bride's eyes were like them in general, and not one in particular. She had their characteristic gentleness in her love and in her look, and no doubt he saw what the Lord meant when He spoke about being *"harmless as doves."*[6] Unlike birds of prey, she had no sharp, threatening gaze, but rather the kindness of her heart being seen in her eyes.

Solomon's commendation said more than it may first appear. Not only did her eyes have a distinct softness, they were particularly so to him.

As far as others were concerned, they were unseen, hidden behind her veil, but he knew more than they did for they were seen by him. If only Israel had looked on their God with like tenderness! Sadly, they often focused on other things, including other gods who, themselves, have eyes, *"but they do not see."*[7] To this day, Paul's words are still true, *"that blindness in part has happened to Israel until the fullness of the Gentiles has come in."*[8] And so it will remain until the scales are lifted from their eyes and *"they will look on* [Him] *whom they pierced."*[9]

His fascination for her eyes caused him to visualise *"the pools in Heshbon by the gate of Bath Rabbim."* What a contrast this evokes! Yes, the loveliness of her eyes conjured up a scene of beauty, but, more than that, it was a scene of beauty against what ultimately became the barren and ungodly background of Moab. Heshbon's history is well documented as a city ruled over by Sihon, king of the Amorites (Josh.3:10; 13:17,21) It was taken by Moses (Num.21:23-26), and became afterwards a Levitical city (Josh.21:39) in the tribe of Reuben (Num.32:37). After the Exile it was taken possession of by the Moabites (Is.15:4; Jer.48:2,45).

The ruins of this town are still seen about 20 miles east of Jordan from the north end of the Dead Sea. There are reservoirs in this district, which are probably the "fishpools" (KJV) referred to in Song 7:4" (Easton's Bible Dictionary). We may wonder what Solomon had in mind, and it's possible that he saw something of the meaning of these names in her. Heshbon is associated with intelligence; and Bath Rabbim can mean daughter of abundance. Two helpful uses of the words *rab or rabīm* are found in Numbers 20:11 when Moses struck the rock and water came out *"abundantly"*; and Psalm 86:5 (RV) tells us that God is *"plenteous"* in His mercy, so her eyes may have exuded the assurance of these inward qualities.

Your hair ... Your temples ... Your head – 4:1, 7:5

In his graphic imagination, he pictured a flock of goats on a hillside like cascading hair, and then, as king, confessed to being captivated by her crowning glory. It seems to indicate that his appreciation of her had grown and felt prompted to move on from speaking about her *"Your hair"* in chapter 4:1 to *"the hair of your head"* in chapter 7:5. Now he combines her hair with the fruitfulness of her Carmel-like head. He also commends "your temples behind your veil are like a piece of a pomegranate," and, once again, he drew attention to the fruitfulness he knew was hidden from others, but reserved and exposed to him. The temples can be a place of weakness and vulnerability, as they proved to be when Jael struck Sisera with a tent peg through the temple,[10] but not so for the bride. To the eyes of her bridegroom, it was the internal glory of her heart and mind that made the external glory of her hair relevant and meaningful. After all, what good is it, if the hair is right and the heart is wrong?

In all this, our attention is being drawn to the delightful thought that her mind was wholly set on him, and that he considered her temples to be places of beauty with the strength and uprightness of a good mind behind them. This certainly couldn't be said about Israel to whom God had to say, *"I know the things that come into your mind."*[11] No matter how veiled their thoughts were to others, He could read the workings of their minds. This was what David wanted to impress on Solomon when he assured him, *"As for you, my son Solomon, know the God of your father, and serve Him with a loyal heart and with a willing mind; for the LORD searches all hearts and understands all the intent of the thoughts."*[12] There seems no doubt, that what God wanted to see in him, he, in turn, wanted to see in his bride.

And is it not so between Christ and us? How vulnerable are our minds? Could there be anything better than to have *"Set your mind on things above,"*[13] but how "set" are they on Him?

> In Him I see the Godhead shine,
> Christ for me, Christ for me;
> He is the majesty divine,
> Christ for me, Christ for me;
> The Father's well-beloved Son,
> Co-partner of His royal throne,
> Who bore the guilt of man alone,
> Christ for me, Christ for me.
> (Richard Jukes)

Robert Murray McCheyne summed up what our spiritual aspiration should be, and he lived it until God called him home when he was only 29 years old: "Remember Jesus for us is all our righteousness before a holy God, and Jesus in us is all our strength in an ungodly world. He justifies sinners who have no righteousness, sanctifies souls that have no holiness. Let Jesus bear your whole weight. Remember, He loves to be the only support of your soul. There is nothing that you can possibly need but you will find it in Him." In his commentary on Colossians 3:2, John MacArthur shares what someone said of McCheyne: "He learned to live in the heavenlies to reach souls on earth. He was fulfilling the command of Romans 12:2, *'Do not be conformed to this world, but be transformed by the renewing of your mind.'*"

Your teeth ... Your lips ... your mouth – 4:2, 3; 7:9

Having spoken of how her eyes revealed the inward feelings of her heart, and how her hair and temples displayed the inner workings of her mind, he now moved on to depict how she communicated these. Only once in the Song, chapter 5:16, she called him her "friend," and speaking of friendship in Proverbs 18:24, Solomon laid out the ground rules that, *"A man who has friends must himself be friendly."* The fruit of true friendship will be seen in the genuineness of one's feelings, in their attitudes to varying circumstances, and in healthy communication. Nothing is fruitless in true friendship. It is single-hearted, not double-minded or double-tongued. Their word is their bond. This was all part of the Shulamite's bridal health-check. There was no corruption in her heart and mind, and no decay in her mouth. Sometimes, there can be disengagement between what the mind thinks and what the tongue says, but no longer with her. To her beloved's satisfaction, there was nothing that would prevent the fragrance of her breath being like apples[14] or remove the evidence of being with him. So it should be for us, too! By sitting under the apple tree and feeding on his fruitfulness, she would carry away his fragrance. So also will those who spend time in the company of Christ.

Just as doves were clean birds, and symbols of purity, so also were her teeth. They were like a flock of shorn sheep that had come up from the washing, so they were carrying nothing of the world's contamination. In dental language, her teeth were perfectly paired, so her bite was as pure and orderly as her bearing and her body. She was what God longed for Israel to be, yet they were not averse to backbiting, as Aaron and Miriam were to Moses in Numbers 12:1, 2. It wasn't long after Israel had been newly redeemed through the Passover lamb, and then the miraculous opening of the Red Sea, that Israel had Massah and Meribah named after their tempting and quarrelling. They were the wrong sort of landmarks to be leaving behind.

To our own sadness and cost, Christians can be guilty of this, too. There are landmarks throughout Christian history of differences that led to disputes, with disputes leading on to division, and some division on to departure. Paul's warning in Galatians 5:15 can be as applicable today as it ever was, *"But if you bite and devour one another, beware lest you be consumed by one another!"* We do well to remember that we are intended to feed one another, not feed on one another! The bride's lips were "like a strand of scarlet" or "a scarlet thread" (ESV). It was her *kᵉ chūt hashānī*, similar in nature to Rahab's *tiqwat chūt hashānī* – line of scarlet cord – that she bound in her window.[15] Rahab's *tiqwat* or *tiqvah* was her hope and expectation, and, even today, the National Anthem of Israel is called 'Hatikvah.' The bride carried her scarlet thread wherever she went, and is a lovely figure of believers sharing their hope in what they say to others. David was concerned about those who defiantly spoke with flattering lips, while saying, *"Our lips are our own; who is lord over us?"*[16] Far from being like this, we would say to our Beloved, the Lord Jesus, *"Grace is poured upon your lips,"*[17] while seeking to apply Solomon's words to ourselves, *"He who loves purity of heart and has grace on his lips, the king will be his friend."*[18]

> May we learn from this great story
> All the arts of friendliness,
> Truthful speech and honest action,
> Courage, patience, steadfastness;
> How to master self and temper,
> How to make our conduct fair;
> When to speak and when be silent,
> When to do and when forbear.

(W.C. Piggott)

Complimenting her for having a *"mouth [that] is lovely,"* he really was saying that her speech was suitable and appropriate. He had no fear of her detracting from her beauty when she opened her mouth, and the Lord should be able to depend on us to *"Let no corrupt word proceed out of [our] mouth, but what is good for necessary edification, that it may impart grace to the hearers."*[19] First, grace on our lips, then grace on their ears; in our speaking, and then on their hearing. Our speech has to be *always "with grace,"*[20] not only in what we say, but in how we say it.

Your neck ... your two breasts – 4:4, 5; 7:3, 4

Once again, we learn that beauty doesn't imply fragility. Just as *"Strength and beauty are in His sanctuary,"*[21] so the bride has both. Between her strength of mind and tenderness of heart, her neck announced her readiness for burden bearing in whatever regal responsibilities lay ahead. It also showed, like Nehemiah's wall around Jerusalem, that she was not only like a wall, but that she was like the strongest part of it represented in its towers. However, lest we jump to the conclusion that she is some sort of superwoman who is prepared for the most robust defence of the place she has been given by her bridegroom, she adds, *"And my breasts are the towers thereof."*[22] She was all for security, but she also was all for sensitivity. Devotion was her defence! This is one thing we are sure to learn: our devotion to Christ will determine how we will defend what is His.

To his delight, she had a heart for the place where he fed his flock among the lilies, and therefore he saw her affections as being set there by saying, "Your two breasts are like two fawns, the twins of a gazelle, which feed among the lilies." It was her way of saying that her heart's longing was to be in the right pasture with the right pastor. He was her King. He also was her shepherd. She knew he would lead, and she knew he would feed. This is an admirable combination, and she gives a lifelong lesson to all believers, that our need to be led is always coupled to our need of being fed. Loyalty through love and vitality through learning always go together, otherwise the will can never be seen in our walk.

Your feet – 7:1

There is something seriously amiss, and most unusual, when a newborn lamb doesn't want to feed. It happens. Even when the ewe's best attempts to stir interest fail, shepherd hands will take over to give much-needed attention and to bottle-feed. As this is being typed, two lambs with the mother ewe are being kept close to our house. One of them was born with joint-ill and its first month is such a challenge for its stability that it struggles to keep upright. Observant shepherds will be quick to spot cases of this and know how to treat it, and so must those who have pastoral care for God's flock. Spiritual lameness reveals itself very quickly, and leaders must be quick to help a young Christian to gain stability and strength. As we noticed earlier, the Shulamite had her own problem with stability, and it doesn't go unnoticed that there is no mention of her feet until we reach the opening verse of chapter 7. In chapter 4, he began at her head; in chapter 7, he started with her feet, and we may ask, "Why?"

The careful reader will have spotted that the word "walk" doesn't appear anywhere in the Song, so it doesn't fit neatly into a library of 'How to' books that focus on the Christian's walk and work. It's a lovely Song that focuses on the heart, on what we should 'be' for God rather than on what we should 'do.' She made the elementary mistake of assuming she was ready to walk when she said, "Draw me," in chapter 1, but he knew she wasn't ready until he shaped her way and spoke about her feet in chapter 7, and we learn from seeing how timely it was for her to hear 'his description of her.'

TRANSITION

"The winter is past, the rain is over and gone."

Brought from winter into springtime, (Song 2:11)
Out of darkness into light,
Out of bondage into freedom,
Out of silence to recite,
By love's awakening, sublime
Views of him that fill her sight.

Eyes not satisfied by seeing (Eccl.1:8)
Fading vision, growing dim,
Ears not satisfied by hearing
In this silent interim;
Lips not satisfied by speaking
Long to voice those words, *"Let him."* (Song 1:2)

Lit the eyes that once were darkened,
Freed the lips that once were sealed,
Filled the mind that, once so empty,
Had her own self-will revealed.
Then his voice! At last, she hearkened (Song 2:8)
And her emptiness was healed.

Gone the days that were unfruitful,
Lonely days of darker hue;

Now the fig tree has its fulness, (Song 2:13)
And the vine has budded, too, (Song 7:12)
God can see within their nearness
His own love-bond with the Jew. (Ps.148:14)

But He also sees the Saviour
With the bride for whom He died
Being made ready for that moment (Rev.19:7)
When she stands there at His side, (Eph.5:27)
Having seen and heard the present (1 Cor.2:9,10)
Blessings love and grace provide.

7

HER DESCRIPTION OF HIM

"My beloved is white and ruddy,
Chief among ten thousand.
His head is like the finest gold;
His locks are wavy, and black as a raven.
His eyes are like doves by the rivers of waters,
Washed with milk, and fitly set.
His cheeks are like a bed of spices, banks of scented herbs.
His lips are lilies, dripping liquid myrrh.
His hands are rods of gold set with beryl.
His body is carved ivory inlaid with sapphires.
His legs are pillars of marble set on bases of fine gold.
His countenance is like Lebanon,
Excellent as the cedars. His mouth is most sweet,
Yes, he is altogether lovely.
This is my beloved, and this is my friend,
O daughters of Jerusalem!"
(Song of Songs 5:10-16)

* * *

Should any Christian need guidance to fulfil Paul's desire in Philippians 3:10, *"That I may know Him,"* there could hardly be a more helpful template than these seven verses in chapter 5 of the Song. It provides an excellent model for a detailed meditation on the Person of Christ, and sets out a line of study that will be richly rewarded by considering each of his twelve features – ten of them set between two opening and closing statements of his overall beauty – and relating them to Him. In this way, her estimation of her beloved will lead us into a deeper contemplation of ours, not least in regard to the preciousness of the body that His God and Father prepared for Him[1] and how He became *"despised and rejected"*[2] by the very nation to whom the language of the Song primarily applies and should have been most greatly loved.

He was everything to her, yet Israel was unmoved as Jerusalem ripened for the judgment of God, as Jeremiah lamented, *"Is it nothing to you, all you who pass by? Behold and see if there is any sorrow like my sorrow, which has been brought on me, which the LORD has afflicted me in the day of His fierce anger."*[3] Nor were they moved when the same question could have been asked, as the rejected Messiah hung on a cross with the full consent of their unmerciful cries and merciless leaders.[4] Having been regarded as *"My servant"*[5] by God, whose *"fame went out among the nations because of* [their] *beauty,"*[6] they descended into being described as showing *"hostility from sinners"*[7] toward the true Bridegroom.

My beloved is white and ruddy

Before presenting her individual appreciation of his virtues, it was as if she stood back to survey him and treasure him in his entirety. Then, after describing the artistry of each part, she stood back once again to unveil the signed canvas of Solomon in all his glory. He was dazzling white (Heb. *tsach*), like the Nazirites in Lamentations 4:7 who were "*brighter* [Heb. *tsachū*] *than snow.*" They also were "ruddy" (Heb. from *ādam*), and her beloved was "ruddy" (Heb. *adōm*). There was something about these consecrated Nazirites, as if they were men of two worlds: white, in their holiness for God, yet ruddy as descendants of Adam. Solomon was like this, too, but he was only a shadow of One who was to come, Jesus of Nazareth: white, because He has the perfect purity of being truly God; and ruddy, because He has the perfect humanity of being truly Man.

Solomon never showed any more than what she saw in him; unlike our Beloved whose "*face shone like the sun, and His clothes became white as the light*"[8] when He was transfigured. Whatever man's description of Him might be, whether by sight or by faith, there is always more glory to Him than anyone has yet seen. Israel crucified "*the Lord of glory,*"[9] completely rejecting the unique whiteness of His divine purity, even when challenged, "*Do you say of Him whom the father sanctified and sent into the world, 'You are blaspheming,' because I said, 'I am the Son of God'?*"[10] They also rejected His manhood when they confronted Pilate: "*If you let this Man go, you are not Caesar's friend. Whoever makes himself a king speaks against Caesar.*"[11] To them, He was neither white nor ruddy! The bride had no difficulty in attaching both words to her beloved, and we have none in seeing their imagery fulfilled in the Saviour. Our eyes are fixed on One who would be minimised if we called Him "*Chief among ten thousand.*" However, with infinitely more right than the Shulamite, we can truly say, "*He is altogether lovely.*"

His head ... his locks – 5:2,11

With their spiritual history behind them, the people of God should have had no hesitation in understanding the bride's depiction of her bridegroom's glory by seeing his head as being *"like finest gold."* They also should have had no hesitation in recalling the golden glory of the tabernacle and temple, yet whole generations lost sight of the glory of the divine mind. The Shulamite's bridal vision ought to have rekindled the nation's recognition of God's will for them, but synchronising theirs with His was a recurring problem. In their blindness, they failed to see that the mind of Christ was at one with the mind of God. They missed its oneness, and therefore were unable to see its holiness, omniscience and willingness. With no concept of His delight in doing His Father's will, they never understood that He was the answer to Psalm 40:7-8, *"Behold, I have come – In the volume of the book it is written of Me – to do your will, O God."*[12] Even in the darkest hours of Gethsemane, He never lost sight of this, and was able to say, *"Nevertheless, not My will, but Yours, be done,"*[13] and faced the cross in such perfect harmony with the mind of God, He was able to say, *"I have finished the work which You have given Me to do.*[14]

<blockquote>
Grateful incense this ascending
Ever to the Father's throne;
Every knee to Jesus bending,
All the mind of heaven is one.
</blockquote>

<blockquote>
All the Father's counsels claiming
Equal honours to the son;
All the Son's effulgence beaming
Makes the Father's glory known.
(J.N. Darby)
</blockquote>

Such was the bridegroom's thoughtfulness toward his bride that he stood knocking (Heb. from *dāphaq*) at her door with the intention of awakening a response from her. Jacob drew from the same word in Genesis 33:13 (KJV) when he appealed to Esau, *"My lord knoweth that the children are tender, and the flocks and herds with young are with me: and if men should overdrive them one day, all the flock will die."* Jacob was being considerate toward the livestock who were suckling, knowing that to overdrive them could threaten the lives of the flock and any unborn lambs. The bridegroom, however, wanted to move his bride by quickening her pace, and in that caring sense wanted to "overdrive" her.

He also was like Jacob, as he stood at her door with his head and dew-soaked hair showing the evidence of his efforts. Israel could have recalled how he reasoned with Laban, *"There I was! In the day the drought consumed me, and the frost by night, and my sleep departed from my eyes."*[15] It was heart-rending for dear Jacob as he added, *"Unless the God of my father, the God of Abraham and the Fear of Isaac, had been with me, surely now you would have sent me away empty-handed. God has seen my affliction and the labor of my hands, and rebuked you last night."* Undoubtedly, the heart of the bridegroom was affected, too, by his bride's sloth, and his black, bushy hair bore its own witness.

His vigour had been spurned; all his efforts were in vain, yet it was little in comparison to Israel's rejection of the Saviour. Isaiah says, *"He was led as a lamb to the slaughter,"*[16] but Acts 8:32 tells us, *"He was led as a sheep to the slaughter; and as a lamb before its shearer is silent, so He opened not His mouth."* It would be the utmost cruelty to shear a lamb, yet this was how the Lamb of God was treated in return for all His efforts. He came that *"The people who sat in darkness* [would see] *a great light, and upon those who sat in the region and shadow of death Light has dawned,"*[17] yet they led Him out to darkness of Calvary.

> Lamb of God for sinners wounded,
> Sacrifice which cancels guilt;
> None shall ever be confounded
> Who on him their hopes have built.
> (T. Kelly)

Throughout the book of Revelation, John refers to Him as the *arnion*, the little or young Lamb. In this, He is ageless in the vigour that took Him to the cross, yet He is coequal with *"the Ancient of Days."*[18] It's in the same character as the eternal, pure, kingly Judge that we see Him in Revelation 1; firstly, as He walks among the seven churches to give His judgment of them, and then as the One through whom this world will be judged. Now his hair is depicted as white: the Holy One who was born to be Saviour, still the Holy One in judgment!

His eyes ... His cheeks ... His lips ... His mouth

The bride had a great affection for her beloved's face, and so do believers as eyes of faith look on our Lord Jesus Christ. His were the eyes that looked on the rich young ruler who ran to Him, "Then Jesus, looking at him, loved him."[19] On another day, "When He saw the multitudes, He was moved with compassion for them."[20] They were shepherd-less, and the good Shepherd looked on them with eyes like doves. As the cock crowed a second time after Peter's threefold denial of the Saviour, "The Lord turned and looked"[21] on him with the same look that accompanied His earlier words, "But I have prayed for you."[22] His eyes were like doves in their melting look, and His lips were like lilies in their glory, yet dripping with sorrow. Whether for the mourning individual, like the widow at Nain, or the city of Jerusalem as a whole, He could have said like Jeremiah, "My eyes bring suffering to my soul because of all the daughters of my city."[23] How ready He was to show His dove-like look and His lily-like lips entered into the guilt and grief of others!

In return, they blindfolded the eyes that were like doves, spat on the cheeks that were like a bed of spices, plucked the hair from them and struck Him.[24] In spite of it all, He never once retaliated. *"When He was reviled, [He] did not revile in return; when He suffered, He did not threaten:"*[25] Even His silence revealed the glory of His lips! It was said of Him, *"No man ever spoke like this Man!"*[26] and others could have added that no one ever looked on them like this Man. The reason is, that no one else had eyes and lips and mouth that belonged to a head that was like the finest gold. It was the divine head that caused those eyes to see the way they did, and His lips and mouth to convey the glory of the divine mind.

On the cross, amid such contradiction, He spoke with lips that were like lilies. Pleading for the guilty, He said, *"Father, forgive them"*;[27] providing for His own, He looked on His mother and John and said, *"Woman, behold your son!"* and to the disciple, *"Behold your mother!"*[28] In response to a dying criminal, He gave that gracious promise, *"Assuredly, I say to you, today you will be with Me in Paradise."*[29] Besides these personal messages, He added the glory of Scripture by saying, *"I thirst,"*[30] and He never said, *"It is finished!"* until He knew *"they had fulfilled all that was written concerning Him."*[31] It was only then that they took Him down from the cross – living soldiers controlled by a dying Man! – that through redeeming grace He also might look upon us.

<blockquote>
I saw One hanging on a tree,
In agony and blood,
Who fixed His languid eyes on me,
</blockquote>

As near His cross I stood.

Sure, never to my latest breath,
Can I forget that look;
It seemed to charge me with His death,
Though not a word He spoke.
(John Newton)

His hands ... His body ... His legs

Two scriptures seem appropriate, as we set 'Her description of him' alongside 'His description of her' and apply them to our union with Christ. The first is Colossians 2:3, *"In whom are hidden all the treasures of wisdom and knowledge"*; and the second is 2 Corinthians 4:7, *"We have this treasure in earthen vessels, that the excellence of the power may be of God and not of us."* Their observation and deep appreciation of each other allowed the Shulamite and Solomon to share the virtues of his name, and the same is true of those who form the Saviour's bride. Together we laud the value of Christ, and the value of being in Christ. She had much to say of him, and he had much to say about her. As we do this, it will begin as the fruit of communion and fellowship with Him, and end as the fruit of lips[32] in worship through Him.

Rings of gold were not unknown to the tribes of Israel, as we will consider in the next chapter, and their particular link with her beloved's hands is very meaningful. She was no stranger to them and valued the attention he gave through them: *"His left hand is under my head, and his right hand embraces me."* She rested in the solace of his supportive left hand, and was secure in the strong clasp of his right. So it was from the early part of the Song, and so it was at the end for she spoke of them in chapter 2:6 and again in 8:3. It was as if he were her servant in his left,

75

yet giving all the confidence and strength from the son of the right hand. It was his hand that reached out to her in chapter 5:4 and was left empty, but, as he later thought of her stature as the palm tree, he contemplated taking hold of its branches.[33] What a perfect example of how our lives should rely and rest in the hands of our Beloved, and that He should be able to take possession of our evident growth and progress!

He is *"the Son of God, who loved me and gave Himself for me,"*[34] and Hebrews 10:10 gives the full cost: He did it *"through the offering of* [His] *body."* There had never been a crucifixion like it for His was a perfect body; the perfect residence and repository of the perfect nature: God manifested in the flesh.[35] There had never been a transaction like it. Others were bearing the punishment of their own sin and guilt; He bore the punishment for ours. When they breathed their last, the purpose of their death was over; but for Him, when the purpose of His death was over, He breathed His last.[36] They were emaciated, broken, and devalued. He was disfigured, unbroken, and, in resurrection, as valuable as ever. The nature that indwelt the incarnation's Infant, still filled the ascension's Man!

At the beginning of this chapter, we thought of how our expressed aim might be to say, *"that I may know Him,"* and the bride helps us to see what this entails. She thought of her beloved as being *"overlaid with sapphires"* (RV). It was her way of saying that she not only knew what was on him, she also knew what was in him. This indicates knowledge at its best. We know nothing of the Saviour's physical features, but we must be thinking of His inward attributes when we say, "that I may know Him." In making this our aim, every Christian should know that the resemblance of Christ is the pleasure of God.

To do this, we need to walk with Him. An old saying on a colleague's desk could be suitably applied to our walk: 'It's not the number of hours you put in that counts, but what you put into the hours.' How true! For us, it's not the number of years, but the number of steps. Unlike other religions, Christianity has no mantras or mottos, and sad it is when such words are used to describe our spiritual aim. A mantra is defined in the Oxford Dictionary as – "(originally in Hinduism and Buddhism) a word or sound repeated to aid concentration in meditation." As for its spiritual purpose, a "mantra is said to quiet the habitual fluctuations of our consciousness and then steer consciousness toward its source in the Self." How sad! It directs the seeker to "Self." For this reason, the Christian has a mandate that directs each of us to Christ: *"For to this you were called, because Christ also suffered for us, leaving us an example, that you should follow His steps."*[37] It was because of the full value of His sin-bearing body that God *"laid **on** Him the iniquity of us all,"*[38] and that He bore them *"**in** His own body."*[39]

As far as the bride was concerned, her beloved's legs were like pillars of marble: pillars being upright and strong, marble (Heb. *shēsh*) being white. Once again, this held meaning for the Jew, since the word *shēsh* also was used for the fine linen in the tabernacle. Their forebears saw it in the hangings of its courtyard, as it stood between the people and the service of a righteous and holy God. The only way in was by the gate *"of blue, purple, and scarlet thread, and fine woven linen."*[40] The Lord Jesus Christ is our only way to God, both in salvation and in service, and we are privileged to walk with Him.

Apart from having legs like pillars, the bride thought of her beloved's feet as being like "bases of fine gold." The King James Version translates from the Hebrew word *eden* as "sockets," but while there were sockets of silver and copper in the tabernacle, this is the only time we read of sockets of gold in Scripture. The word *'eden* is closely associated with 'adōn, from which we have Adonāy for the Lord, as in Psalm 71:16, "*I will go in the strength of the Lord GOD – Adonāy Yahweh.* What a God-honouring and Christ-exalting way to walk! And we do it as we respond to this call, "*As you have therefore received Christ Jesus the Lord, so walk in Him, rooted and built up in Him and established in the faith, as you have been taught, abounding in it with thanksgiving.*"[41]

His countenance is like Lebanon

Many versions say, "His appearance is like Lebanon," as a preferable translation of *mar'ēhūto* to convey the thought of her overall view of him. In comparison to her being like a palm tree, he is like cedars in their towering majesty. In his giving, he is as accessible as the apple tree, but like the cedar in his grandeur. Her consideration of him is choice, since it begins at his head, takes us down to his feet, and then lifts our gaze much higher than when she started. May the same be said about us, that, in our expressed appreciation of the Lord Jesus Christ, we draw others to Him in his headship, bring them to His feet, that from there their gaze might soar upwards until they are overwhelmed by the One who "*is altogether lovely.*"

WHAT IS YOUR BELOVED?
Very image of God's Person, (Heb.1:3)
Brightness beaming from His heart;
Very God in all His Being, (1 Tim.3:16)
Very God in every part.
In HIs fine golden head defined
Christ of the eternal mind;
And with His eyes, His lips and mouth (Jn 3:11)
Conveys rich eternal truth.

78

Eyes that felt and showed compassion, (Matt.9:36)
Lips that still reveal His heart, (Ps.45:2)
Mouth that uttered words of comfort (Lk.7:13)
Find their perfect counterpart:
For the glory of His vision,
And the glory of His word, (Jn 4:26)
All belong to perfect Godhead –
Glorious King and glorious Lord! (Rev.19:16)

Yet that glory condescended
In a body, full of grace (Tit.2:11)
And the riches of God's goodness, (Rom.2:4)
Came to suffer in our place. (1 Pet.3:18)
Richer far than any sapphire; (2 Cor.8:9)
Rarer, more than ivory's price
For its worth is cherished only
When obtained by sacrifice. (Eph.5:2)

Flesh and blood, like any other, (Heb.2:14)
But the myst'ry of God's plan (Col.2:2)
Is the treasure in that body: (Col.2:3)
Truly God, yet truly Man.
Eyes blindfolded, mocked and smitten, (Lk.22:64)
Stricken cheeks and plucked-off hair; (Is.50:6)
Yet His body lost no riches
Though they pierced it with a spear (Jn 19:34)

His the hands that measure waters (Is.40:12)
And the distant upper spheres;
And He holds all things together, (Col.1:17)
As th'Eternal spans earth's years;

Yet He reached and healed the leper (Matt.8:2,3)
With His precious golden touch,
And He reaches out to sinners
Knowing who will love Him much. (Lk.7:47)

He walks on the wings of the wind, (Ps.104:3)
And on waves in Galilee; (Matt.14:25)
And He makes His way in the skies, (Ps.68:34)
As He makes His path in the sea. (Ps.77:19)
With legs like pillars of marble,
His walk is upright and pure;
There is purpose in His going, (Acts 2:23)
God's pleasure in them is sure. (Ps.147:10)

But they held those feet and nailed them, (Ps.22:16)
Pierced through on Calvary's tree,
That to us they might also be golden,
Like sockets of Lordship to be. (Ex.26:19)
Outstanding among ten thousand, (Song 5:10)
There is none as lovely as He: (Song 5:16)
And then, with Him in His glory,
His face, at last, we shall see. (Ps.17:15)

Arise, My bride, it's the morning! (Song 2:10)
The winter is past and gone. (Song 2:11)
The Beloved's voice will call us,
And to His presence be drawn.
We shall be there in His likeness (1 Jn 3:2)
Forever in regions of bliss.
We'll praise His Name at His coming,
Rejoicing that we are His. (Song 6:3)

8

PRIESTLINESS

"His hands are as gold rings set with the beryl:
his belly is as bright ivory overlaid with sapphires."

"My dove, my undefiled is but one;
she is the only one of her mother,
she is the choice one of her that bare her.
The daughters saw her, and called her blessed;
yea, the queens and the concubines, and they praised her."
(Song of Songs 5:14; 6:9 RV)

* * *

In a song about the king, we would expect kingly references, and there are. She speaks of the king's chambers and table in chapter 1 that would bring her into the blessing of his majestic resting place and the fulness of his provision. Then she describes the stately parade for his ornate palanquin (a portable couch carried on two poles) in chapter 3 escorted by sixty mighty men who encircled it. The whole scene is glorious, including Solomon wearing the crown *"with which his mother crowned him on the day of his wedding."* Finally, in chapter 7, the bride's flowing hair binds him to her in sheer fascination.

While all this meant much to the couple, its imagery also held meaningful analogies for Israel and for the present-day believer's enjoyment of Christ. There is much here from which Israel should have anticipated the King who came to them, not on an elaborate sedan couch, but on a donkey with her colt, yet *"crowned with glory and honour"* by His Father.[1] However, most of them missed this as being the fulfilment of all their messianic hopes, and still do, but they also seem to have missed the priestly inferences in the Song. They love the City of David, yet they despised his greater Son and led him outside its gates to be crucified. To this day, they remain without a monarch and without anything that relates to priestly service. In another bridal book, Hosea describes this barren emptiness: *"For the children of Israel shall abide many days without king or prince, without sacrifice or sacred pillar, without ephod or teraphim. Afterward the children of Israel shall return and seek the LORD their God and David their king. They shall fear the LORD and His goodness in the latter days."*[2]

A Holy Nation

Throughout the Song, there are various references that should have reminded Israel of her national identity and priestly association as the people of God. For example: such words as, *"watchmen ... keepers ... no spot."*

*Watchmen of the walls - 5:7 ESV

Even the thought of walls should have triggered affection for the most important wall of all, around Jerusalem, with its gates, bolts and bars, and towers. When God invited His people to *"Walk about Zion, and go all around her; count her towers; mark well her bulwarks; consider her palaces; that you may tell it to the generation following,"*[3] He must have expected them to take note of how much they owed to the watchmen on the wall and to the keepers of the gates. God certainly did, and His people should always learn to appreciate what He appreciates! When He listed some names in 1 Chronicles 9:19, He made a point of adding, *"Their fathers had been keepers of the entrance to the camp of the LORD."* They fulfilled what He went on to call in verse 22, *"their trusted office."* Each generation provided its men for the purpose, and what a lesson this is that we don't lean on past protectors of the faith without producing God-honouring replacements in each generation.

These men were set by divine appointment for a divine need. Appointing them was God's work: *"I have set watchmen on your walls, O Jerusalem"*[4]; fulfilling their appointment was their work. The word *shāmar* suggests they were to be like the impenetrable barrier of a thorn hedge, men who gave heed to things that should never be given up by guarding and protecting what was inside from what was outside. If the Song had stirred such appreciation among the leaders of Israel, long years of disobedience, captivity and shame could have been prevented. Alas, the Lord Himself summed up their callous disregard. *"O Jerusalem, Jerusalem, the city that kills the prophets and stones those sent to her! How often I wanted to gather your children together, just as a hen gathers her brood under her wings, and you would not have it!"*[5]

In contrast to this, God gave the other side of the same coin through

Jeremiah: *"The prophets prophesy falsely, and the priests rule by their own power; and My people love to have it so."*[6] What a sad day it is in any generation when the people of God have what He doesn't want them to have, and do not have what He does want them to have! It happened with the bride, it happened with Israel, and we need to make sure it doesn't happen with us.

*My own vineyard - 1:6

From beginning to end, the Song's repeated mention of the vineyard should have prompted fresh affection among the people of Israel for the One who *"brought a vine out of Egypt."*[7] God's intention was always for the fruitfulness of His people and, after speaking of His bridal bond with them in Jeremiah 2:2-3, He described them as *"a noble vine"* in v.21, yet Hosea saw them as *"empty."*[8] How sad that what God had seen as *sorēq*, choice, was changed to *bāqaq*, because it had *"failed"*[9] and become *"void"*![10] Some versions translate *bāqaq* as *"luxuriant"* and this may give conflicting impressions of what Hosea meant, but his picture is of Israel pouring all her energies into what appears to be good growth, but in reality was fruitless. The Lord's words for their emptiness and apparent luxuriance were, *"Nothing but leaves."*[11]

If only they had resolved their emptiness, as the Shulamite did by recapturing her love for her beloved, but even centuries later, Isaiah penned *"A song of my Beloved regarding His vineyard."* In it, God asks, *"And now, O inhabitants of Jerusalem and men of Judah, judge, please, between Me and My vineyard. What more could have been done to My vineyard that I have not done to it? Why then, when I expected it to bring forth good grapes, did it bring forth wild grapes?"*[12] The main reason was, of course, that they thought *"wild grapes"* and *"leaves"* were good enough for God. It was very different when Elisha discovered *"death in the pot"* because poisonous *"wild gourds"* had been shredded into the stew. Immediately, he recognised that wild gourds were not acceptable for the sons of the prophets, yet Israel didn't want to admit there was death in the pot by offering wild grapes to God.

*The fig - 2:13

Apart from Solomon's knowledge of trees, God's people would have known the significance of the vine and the fig tree. Both were symbols of them as a nation, applied to them by God Himself, so they should almost have venerated the very mention of them in the Song. How could they miss them? The answer is simple: they had become so blind to the things of God, and so deaf to the voice of God, that none of it registered. As He would say through Isaiah at a later date, *"The whole head is sick, and the whole heart faints."*[13] As with the walls of Jerusalem, Israel had one true *Shomēr* who protected and guarded them as their Keeper, by day and night,[14] and would not give them up.[15] In Solomon's only mention of the fig tree in his parables (Proverbs), he made the statement, *"Whoever keeps the fig tree will eat its fruit,"*[16] yet there were no figs on the fig tree when the Lord saw it and was hungry. How their emptiness failed the Keeper of the fig tree!

However, all was not lost. As He walked among them, and tasted the bitter fruit of their empty hearts and minds, faithful individuals came to Him. One was Nathaniel, *"an Israelite indeed,"* – a true man of the rule of God! – and the Lord surprised him by saying, *"Before Philip called you, when you were under the fig tree, I saw you."*[17] Was that a natural tree or spiritually figurative? Well, perhaps, both. There may have been a fig tree under which he found shade, but it's just as likely that the omniscient Lord was letting him know that He recognised genuine fruit from the *"fig tree"* nation. Zacchaeus was another example. It was from a sycamore fig tree that the Lord called him as an example of the fruit He had come *"to seek and to save"* and to whom He gave the promise, *"Today salvation has come to this house, because he also is a son of Abraham."*[18] In other words, a man of faith.

*Honey and milk - 4:11

This is an unusual phrase, especially when we think of *"Honey and milk* [being] *under your tongue."* By itself, it's difficult to understand, but less so when we link it with other scriptures that include the word *tachat* for *"under."* Speaking of the wicked, Psalm 10:7 says, *"His mouth is full of cursing and deceit and oppression, under his tongue is trouble and iniquity."* Psalm 66:17 paints a very different picture: *"I cried to Him with my mouth, and He was extolled with* [tachat – under] *my tongue."* Another example is found in Psalm 140:3 RV, *"They have sharpened their tongues like a serpent; adders' poison is under their lips."* In all these cases, including the last being cited in Romans 3:13, the implication seems to be that what is under the tongue is the content and character of what the person is about to say.

If the heart is full of lies, they will fill the mouth and spill out when the person speaks. On the other hand, when thoughts that exalt the Lord flow from the heart and mind, the tongue will be ready to speak them. It's in this sense we believe that *"honey and milk were under her tongue."* Her words were befitting in the ears of the king, just as Israel's should have been in the ears of God. Those who live in the land that flows with milk and honey[19] should have appropriate thoughts and words that flow in appreciation to the God who brought them there!

In contrast to the mouth of sinners, her lips, speech and appetite were all a reflection of Canaan. There was comeliness about her mouth, which was in character with the land, and with the Lord, and this was another reminder of Israel's precious link with the place of priestly service.

A priestly people

The Song's relevance to Israel as *"a holy nation"* continues in the accompanying thought that they also were *"a kingdom of priests."*[20] Whenever the tabernacle was set up, the Levites formed a priestly zone around it, and they represented the whole nation that encamped around them and it. This was, in one sense, a priestly barricade and guard for God's dwelling place and for all the priestly activity that took place within it, and during its transit. In another sense, it also was a region that acted as a priestly precinct around the pure white screen and the actual gateway. Irrespective of the tribe from which each person came to offer at the altar of God, all must pass through the cordon of Levites before accessing the screen by means of the gate. All three were reminders that everyone in the holy nation had a priestly service to fulfil, but also a responsibility to draw near with a real sense of priestly compliance. With all this in mind, we may wonder how the contents of the Song could hold priestly promptings for the people of Israel, and we will find that it is not short of them.

*Rings of gold set with beryl - 5:14 RV

During the bride's careful list of her bridegroom's features, she said, *"His hands are rings of gold."* She thought of his hands at different stages of the Song, and even this should have caused God's people to think of the goodness of His hand toward them. However, it was by describing them as rings of gold that they could have made a valued connection with other important rings of gold in God's Word.

From Exodus 25:12 onward, there are many references to *"rings of gold"*: for the ark of the covenant, table of showbread, the boards, breastplate, altar of incense and pillars. All of them were made so that they could be filled with carrying poles. The purpose of the rings was to make the poles belong to the items of tabernacle furniture: the rings never went forward without the poles, and the poles never went forward without the rings. Likewise, the hands that were like *"rings of gold"* should have been filled, too. Her hands belonged in the hands of her bridegroom, but sadly, she left them empty, and this is exactly what the people of Israel did with God.

She developed such an appreciation of his hands that she added the thought that they were *"set with beryl,"* which is doubly precious. She may have intended only that his golden hands were embellished with gemstones, but her word *"set"* has its own precious meaning for she drew from the same Hebrew word, *mālē'*, that God used in Exodus 25:7 – *"stones to be set in the ephod and in the breastplate."* It includes the thoughts of being entirely filled and consecrated, as in 1 Chronicles 29:5 when King David asked, *"Who then is willing to consecrate himself this day to the LORD?"* His actual phrase, *lᵉmallo'wt yādō*, can mean to fill the hand, but the implications are much more akin to being consecrated by his *"service"* (KJV) or, as translated in 2 Chronicles 7:6, the Levites' *"ministry."*

There is so much here to convict Jews, but we take the lesson to ourselves for it speaks loudly to us too. Our Saviour's hands are as rings of gold, first of all from the point of view that all who believe are securely in His grasp for *"they shall never perish; neither shall anyone snatch them out of [His] hand."*[21] Through our salvation, our lives are firmly in the hands of our Beloved, but are His hands being filled by us in service? As we think of this, we hear Paul's words to Archippus in Colossians 4:17

and take them to ourselves, *"Take heed to the ministry which you have received in the Lord, that you may fulfil it."* If we do this, our hands will be filled, and we will fill His too!

In Exodus 26:6, God also designed *"clasps of gold"* and they achieved a similar purpose. By means of fifty clasps, ten tabernacle curtains were held together in two sets of five. The word *"clasps"* comes from a Hebrew word which means "to stoop," and what a lovely picture this gives of the condescension of the Lord Jesus as He stooped into humanity that He might unite us in testimony for Himself. The curtains were "coupled," and that means they were brought together into fellowship with each other. What a lovely indication that, through His "stoop" we are united with Him in glorious service. Other aspects of priestliness are seen in –

*Priestly attire - 4:3; 6:7

Having become so impressed by her fruitfulness, the beloved speaks twice in a similar manner. Altogether he saw her temperament and character as a garden in which her *"plants are an orchard of pomegranates."* Some time later he also said, *"Like a piece of pomegranate are your temples."* The word "pomegranate" comes from a Hebrew word meaning "exalted" or "upright," and therefore is used for the fruitfulness that exalts priestly relationship and likeness (Ex.28:31-35). There were finely embroidered whole pomegranates on the hemline of the high priest's robe of the ephod and these speak of fruitfulness that is enclosed. The mind of the bride was reserved for her beloved and *"a piece of a pomegranate"* speaks of fruitfulness that is exposed. It suggests that the pomegranate has been broken open or sliced, as if to reveal how fruitful her mind is in all its thoughts, intentions, comprehension and imaginations. Apart from the high priest, there were carved pomegranates on the tops of the two pillars in the temple,[22] so there were reminders of fruitfulness in both the lowest and highest places in the service of God. Perhaps, it's to remind us that lowly thoughts and lofty thoughts come from the same fruitful mind!

It has to do with the character and content of the mind, but also points to its control. As we know, this can be a major battle, but is possible to achieve if we bring *"every thought into captivity to the obedience of Christ."*[23] For this to happen, the word of Christ and the Spirit of Christ need to be effective in us, and then *"The peace of God, which surpasses all understanding, will guard your hearts and minds through Christ Jesus."*[24]

On Lord's Day mornings, it is uplifting to discover how God's people bear the fruitfulness of their Priest by speaking specifically about His worth. Worship will expose what has been enclosed, and what has been concealed will be revealed as the premeditated, prepared thoughts of His priestly people are expressed. When we are together collectively, we ought to be like *"an orchard of pomegranates."* It should be the place of harvested meditation from minds that are set on Christ, and there should be no shortage of fruitful thought ready to be turned into *"the fruit of our lips."*[25] Along with everyone else, He should be able to see *"your plants."*

This word has two very distinct meanings in Hebrew. Firstly, it can mean "plants" being like the development of our meditations from an initial thought, as we have been thinking. That's the positive side. Negatively, the word could be translated "weapon" and it is easy to imagine the unproductive thoughts and speech that can be hurled so abusively like missiles from an unfruitful mind. We can smite with the tongue.[26] Bad speech is the result of bad thoughts, but God looks for *"a garden enclosed."* It is a fruitful enclosure, and reveals itself in worship through fruitful disclosure.

*Priestly activity - 5:10-16

We have already thought of the bride and bridegroom's reference to doves in the Song and their place among the offerings at the altar. As the bride surveyed her beloved with such devoted perception, it was as if the piece of the pomegranate was expressing itself by separating the bull of the burnt offering into its pieces. Leviticus 1 speaks of the head, the pieces, the inwards and the legs, and Leviticus 9:13, ESV speaks of *"piece by piece, and the head."* There was nothing haphazard about giving a burnt offering. It had to be *"cut into its pieces"*, which is very different from being cut into pieces. Anyone could do the latter, but only an ordered mind could do the former!

As for the bride, she was well able to describe him in similar detail from head to foot. She knew him well, so well that she listed six features to do with his head. Could we do that with Christ? Do we know Him *"piece by piece, and the head"*? She also knew what was in him: *"His body is carved ivory inlaid with sapphires."* Theirs was no casual or superficial acquaintance! It was like setting a high value on seeing *"truth in the inward parts"*[27] of the Saviour's perfection. Oh, to know Him so well!

In chapter 7:5, his reference to Carmel would remind a Jew of the meal offering which had *"corn of the fresh ear."*[28] The word *"fresh"* is identical to *"Carmel"* which means *fruitful.* Then, in verses 10-13, her fellowship with him is a reminder of the peace offering. The sin offering can be applied to her times of relapse when she needed restoration, after sorrow had gripped her repentant heart. And there is a hint of the trespass offering language in chapter 8:12 where we read of the fifth part. *"Solomon may have a thousand* [pieces of silver] *and those who tend its fruit two hundred."* In making restitution *"for the harm that he has done,"* *that is in* the sin that has been committed, the offender must add an additional twenty per cent. This is called 'the fifth part' or 'the double tithe' and emphasised the gravity of taking away something that rightly belonged to someone else. David is another example when he slew Goliath with one stone of his five.

When the Lord Jesus Christ fulfilled the trespass offering, he could have borrowed David's words in Psalm 69:4 and said, *"I restored that which I took not away"* (KJV). He restored what was lost through Adam's fall and added more, even though He was not the One who had taken it away. The sinless Christ was treated as guilty and made accountable for our guilt. He brought us into the reality of clearing our indebtedness, into the power of His resurrection, into greater sense of triumph than David, and greater fruitfulness than the bride. The different aspects of His offering can be viewed as follows:

- Leviticus 5:16 – Restitution associated with the fifth part: **INDEBT-EDNESS;**
- Leviticus 23:13 – Resurrection associated with the fifth part: **LIVE-LINESS;**
- 1 Samuel 17:40,49 – Victory associated with the fifth part: **SUCCESS;**
- 1 Kings 6:31 – Access associated with the fifth part: **ACCESS;**
- Song of Songs 8:12 – Reward associated with the fifth part: **FRUIT-FULNESS.**

He also brought us into restored:

- **RELATIONSHIP** – *"He gave the right to become children of God"* (Jn 1:12);
- **LIFE** – *"I have come that they may have life"* (Jn 10:10);
- **PEACE** – *"My peace I give to you"* (Jn 14:27);
- **JOY** – *"My joy may remain in you"* (Jn 15:11);

- **RIGHTEOUSNESS** - *"By one Man's obedience many will be made righteous"* (Rom.5:19);
- **UNION** - *"For you are all one in Christ"* (Gal.3:28);
- **BLESSING** - *"Blessed us with every spiritual blessing"* (Eph.1:3);
- **HOPE** - *"Christ Jesus our hope"* (1 Tim.1:1 RV);
- **GLORY** - *"In bringing many sons to glory"* (Heb.2:10);
- **COMMUNION** - *"Our fellowship is with the Father and with His Son Jesus Christ"* (1 Jn 1:3).

*Priestly anointing - 4:13,14

She was fragrant like the temple, and it was as if she belonged there, which is more than could often be said of God's people. Had she ever thought to ask Solomon if he was describing the holy anointing oil and the incense, he would have replied, "No, I'm describing you." Even so, Jewish minds would absorb what he thought of her and recall the ingredients of the holy anointing oil and incense in Exodus 30:22-38. If only the Lord could do the same with us! We are highly honoured in being helped by the Holy Spirit to bring to God something of the fragrance that Christ Himself brings to Him.

Treasure beyond all telling, Friend when the trusted fail,
Comfort in Jordan's swelling, strength when foes assail,
Rock when the sands are shifting, anchor in storm-tossed sea,
Surety in aimless drifting – all this He is to me.
Joy to the sorrowing spirit, rest after fruitless toil –
Forgiven alone through His merit, sealed by anointing oil:
Light when the dark clouds hover, in the unknown way a Guide:
All this, O matchless Lover, all this and heaven beside.

*Priestly authority - 4:13,16; 7:11-13

What a joy it was to both bride and bridegroom that she was able to speak about her *"pleasant fruits"*! Perhaps it was her way of seeing her own progress as good, better and best. First of all, she was like the enclosed garden that was all for him, then she called for the differing conditions under the influence of winds from north and south to carry the proof of her fragrance to him. It was to her advantage that she had learned it takes contrasting winds to blow before spices flow. Finally, and best of all, she called him to witness the triple evidence of her continuing fruitfulness of buds, blossoms and fruit.

With all three present for his approval, she was a vivid reminder to Israel of their dispute over Aaron that was settled by his rod springing to life with buds, blossoms and ripe almonds, while the rods from other eleven tribes remained lifeless. The miraculous sequence confirmed the right of the Aaronic priestly line, as God's authority was established in a dead rod becoming so alive, and showing all the stages of development. As she walked hand in hand with her beloved in chapter 7:10-13, *"all manner of precious fruits"* (RV) were *"at our gates,"* Israel should have been convicted about their need to engage in the priestly activity of taking baskets of fruit to their priest.[29]

In Christ, we can apply these four aspects of our priestly relationship: ATTIRE, ACTIVITY, ANOINTING and AUTHORITY. By His stooping, we have fellowship with one another, as if clasped by rings of gold. And He fascinates us! Like the bridegroom, He puts in His hand that our hearts might be moved. His left hand is under our heads to support, and His right hand clasps us to Himself. These were the ministries of the hands that were *"as rings of gold,"* and much more so for our Saviour's nail-pierced hands. Will we allow Him to fill our hands, so that we may come and fill His? There is no finer service this side of heaven than to fill the hands that for our sakes are as *"rings of gold."*

FRUIT, BLOSSOM AND BUD

I feast on the fruit that He bears
And O it is sweet to my taste;
The virtues and glories He wears,
The beauties wherewith He is graced.

But still as I study Him more,
And ponder His words and His ways,
New beauties unnoticed before
Are blossoming out to my gaze.

And humbly, yet gladly, I own,
Though daily new glimpses I get,
There's many a glory unknown
That's still in the bud to me yet.

Yet, such is His fulness, and such
The freshness and dew of His youth,
Time's withering hand cannot touch
His treasures of goodness and truth.

He's the Rod and the Branch and the Root,
And still to my wondering soul,
Will bud and will bloom and bear fruit
While the years of eternity roll.
(J.M.S. Tait)

9

COMMUNION

"Return, return, O Shulamite; Return, return, that we may look upon you!

"How beautiful are your feet in sandals, O prince's daughter!"

"I am my beloved's, and his desire is toward me.
Come, my beloved, let us go forth to the field;
Let us lodge in the villages. Let us get up early to the vineyards;
Let us see if the vine has budded,
Whether the grape blossoms are open,
And the pomegranates are in bloom.
There I will give you my love.
The mandrakes give off a fragrance,
And at our gates are pleasant fruits,
All manner, new and old,
Which I have laid up for you, my beloved."
(Song of Songs 6:13; 7:1, 10-13)

* * *

I am my beloved's

J ust as her bridegroom had expressed his affection by calling her *"My dove"* three times, the bride had her own way of expressing hers for him, and she also found three different ways of say it. In chapter 2:16, she thought of him as her possession and of his occupation by saying, *"My beloved is mine, and I am his. He feeds his flock among the lilies."* She then changed the order in chapter 6:3 to put more emphasis on him by thinking of him as her possessor and of his occupation: *"I am my beloved's, and my beloved is mine. He feeds his flock among the lilies."* Finally, any arranging of order was discarded and she became totally absorbed by the realisation that she was possessed and that she was the centre of his attention: *"I am my beloved's, and his desire is toward me."* How wonderful that such a thought should captivate her whole being or, as David said, *"all that is within me."*[1] At last, she had reached the peak of appreciation of her beloved and was altogether ready to go forward with him, and she said these long-awaited words:

Come, my beloved

This is the first time in the Song that she says, *"Come."* She couldn't say it earlier for her mercurial experience wouldn't allow it. In more lethargic times, she had known what it was to lose the sense of his presence that resulted in her having to search and ask for help in finding him. In the relief of uniting, she spoke of seizing him and not slackening her grip, but then discovered the sad truth of Solomon's warning in Proverbs 10:4, *"He who has a slack hand becomes poor."* Before long, she felt the watchmen's harsh treatment as she searched for a second time, and then had to tell the daughters of Jerusalem what to say if they found him before she did.[2]

The whole episode makes us search our own hearts to see if we also have lost sight of our Beloved or risk being on the receiving end of judgmental words and actions. The tragedy is, that we sometimes need to be redirected to Him, and what a relief it is to be restored!

With her struggles over, and these dark times in the past, she now wanted to live in the full enjoyment of his company, and so it was time for her to say, *"Come, my beloved."* Now she was ready to enter into the fulness of his former appeals. Chapter 2:13 was his invitation for her to come; chapter 4:8 was his preparation for her to leave her depths and rise to share his outlook from the heights; but now, in chapter 7:11, they enter into a long-awaited sense of communion and shared vision. All three can be known in Christ, as we "Come" to share in His invitation, vision and communion.

Such words will be on our lips, too, when we realise that we also are possessed by Him and are the object of Divine affection. What a delight to be taken up with the work of the triune God in this matter! Our Beloved is *"the Son of God who loved [us] and gave Himself for [us]"*[3]; and He said to His Father, *"They were Yours, You gave them to Me"*[4]; and the Holy Spirit is the One *"In whom also, having believed, you were sealed with the Holy Spirit of promise."*[5] Sadly, we can live without knowing what He has called us to and thus fail to enter into His grand preparation in 1 Corinthians 2:9 – *"Eye has not seen, nor ear heard, nor have entered into the heart of man the things God has prepared for those who love Him."* This has often been understood as applying to what lies ahead in every believer's glorious future in heaven, but Paul was thinking of all that we can enjoy presently in our daily walk with the Lord. He assures us of this in the next verse: *"But God has revealed them to us through His Spirit,"* as a present experience.

PUBLICLY WALKING TOGETHER: Let us go forth into the field.

So far in the Song, she has said, "Let him" and he has said, "Let me," but neither of them has said, "Let us." Now she says it four times, as if in answer to his fourfold *"Return"* in chapter 6:13. It's also rather noticeable that his descriptions of her have never mentioned her feet. Previously, he had started at her head; but now, in chapter 7, he begins with her feet. Why the change? The reason is that it's only now that her actions correspond with her affections; and she proves that when the heart is won, the feet will follow! There was no doubt that she loved him, and that greatly, but she had known what it was to walk alone.

Twice he came and called,[6] and twice she spurned him. She had given a wonderfully detailed description of her beloved to the daughters of Jerusalem that could only have come from deep affection and clear perception. It was as if she had to let them know how much he meant to her, but they were words without actions. Wonder it is that they never enquired, "If you love him so much, why are you not with him?" She had been lethargic and her activities were out of place, but now everything was as it should be and he began with her feet. She was wearing sandals, so was ready to walk with him! Now she was with him – *"in the field."* There was no secret about it. They had not always been seen in public, but now everyone could see their togetherness. What a lesson on beautiful feet, when the beauty of ours corresponds with the beauty of His![7] It's the value of open witness! If we are going to share our Beloved publicly we will need to do as she did and show the fruit of our communion with Christ to others.

PRIVATELY LIVING TOGETHER: Let us lodge in the villages.

She had known what it was like to dwell alone[8] and her dwelling place had been marked out by her separation *from* him. Her home had been the place of division, *"behind our wall,"* but our Bridegroom wants the inside place, the place of union and communion,[9] and of separation *to* Him. Even though they had a variety of residences – *"in the villages"* – her companion was constant. They changed places, but she never changed partners with each overnight stop.

Among the early questions Jesus was asked by Andrew and John, they said to Him, *"Where are You staying?"* He said to them, *"Come and see."* May what was said of their response that day also be said of our lifelong communion with Him: *"They came and saw where He was staying, and remained with Him."*[10]

> Master, where Thou hast Thy dwelling, fain would I abide,
>   With the sweetness of Thy presence fully satisfied.
>   In that fair abode my spirit breathes her native air;
> Peace that passeth understanding doth surround me there.
>
> Yes, the blessed joy of heaven is my perfect part!
> Strange that lesser things should ever charm my foolish heart;
> Keep me, Master, where Thou dwellest, occupied with Thee,
>   So that body, soul and spirit sanctified may be.
>   (Author unknown)

FRUITFULNESS TOGETHER: Let us get up early to the vineyards.

There's a most welcomed contrast between the opening of the Song and its close. The Shulamite put her confessed failure behind her, *"My own vineyard I have not kept,"*[11] and was now able to boast, *"My own vineyard is before me."*[12] *"Not kept"* means she didn't guard or cherish what was hers. This is a sharp lesson for us when we try to correct the wrongs of others whilst overlooking our own; when we are more concerned about the mote in our brother's eye than with the beam in our own.[13]

She also left behind days of rising alone,[14] now she was rising early with him. *"Let us get up early"* meant rising together. She had been more accustomed to getting up late, but now the day isn't long enough, and it has to be begun with him. What a difference! The victorious life keeps early appointments with God. It was in Cambridge University, England, in 1882 that the world was first given the slogan, 'REMEMBER THE MORNING WATCH.' Students like Hooper and Thornton found their days packed with studies, discussions, etc. Activity was the order of the day. These dedicated men soon discovered a crack in their spiritual armour which, if not closed, would bring disaster. They sought an answer and came up with a scheme - THE MORNING WATCH - the plan of spending the first minutes of the day with God, in prayer and reading the Word. It sealed the crack.

The idea caught fire and "a remarkable period of blessing followed" that culminated in the departure of the Cambridge Seven for missionary service in China. They found getting out of bed was as difficult as it was vital. Thornton invented an automatic cure for laziness: "The vibrations of an alarm clock set fishing tackle in motion, and the sheets, clipped to the line, moved swiftly into the air off the sleeper's body." Thornton wanted so much to get up and meet his God!

In Psalm 5:3, David emphasises the value of this, *"My voice You shall hear in the morning, O LORD; in the morning I will direct it to You, and I will look up."* Another clear example of this is in Psalm 119:147, *"I rise before the dawning of the morning, and cry for help."* The King James Version phrases this quite differently: *"I prevented the dawning of the morning,"* by which it means, not that the psalmist could hinder it, but that he could anticipate it or meet it with God. The Lord Jesus Christ also did this, as Mark 1:35-38 tells us: *"Now in the morning, having risen a long while before daylight, He went out and departed to a solitary place, and there he prayed."* Mark goes on to say that they searched for Him, and when they found Him, He said, *"Let us go."* It's the perfect way to serve God: to pray, and then go, rather than to go before praying!

SEEING TOGETHER: Let us see ... the vine ...the pomegranates.

She had known what it was to see things alone at the beginning of chapter 3, and had expected the seeing of others to come to her aid when she asked what they had seen. His eyes were like doves, and so were hers, therefore her eyes should see as he sees, but she suffered from a kind of myopia that made her see farther by hindsight than with foresight. Is it like that with us? Does our Beloved see what we see? Does He read what we read or watch what we watch? Or does He stand and offer us eye-salve to anoint our eyes, so that we may see as He sees?[15]

As we read the Song, it's easy to see that one defect leads to another, and it soon becomes apparent that her lack of appreciation led on to idleness, unfruitfulness and short-sightedness. It was a malady that affected her, and badly affected the service and testimony of the people of Israel, but it wasn't only an Old Testament problem. Exactly the same link is made in 2 Peter 1:8 and 9. No sooner does Peter finish encouraging us to be thoroughly diligent in adding,

> *"to your faith virtue, to virtue knowledge, to knowledge self-control, to self-control perseverance, to perseverance godliness, to godliness brotherly kindness, and to brotherly kindness love,"* than he spells out the clearest warning. *"For if these things are yours and abound, you will be neither barren nor unfruitful in the knowledge of our Lord Jesus Christ. For he who lacks these things is shortsighted, even to blindness, and has forgotten that he was cleansed from his old sins."*

This isn't simply loss of memory, it's loss of assurance, and, if we let it go, it may not be long until we lose our appreciation too. When this happens, we will lose the fruitfulness of thinking and learning of the Saviour, and this can lead to the tragic conclusion of no longer seeing things the way we used to see them. Some have lost their appreciation of Christ and His saving work, and then have been influenced to see things that are contrary to the gospel, and we would long for the equivalent of the beloved's fourfold *"Return"* to turn them around until they reply with their own fourfold *"Let us."*

"Let us see" also means SEEKING TOGETHER. What did they see? They looked together upon *"bud ... blossom ... bloom,"* all the tokens of prolific fruitfulness. She was walking, dwelling and seeing, in the power of true renewal! She was living with him in a place that was absolutely alive. He had already been to see all these things in preparation for her coming. Now she has entered into the joy of it, but it could only be with him. There is no indication that she could have entered into it on her own. So it is with us. Christ our Saviour sees and knows all about the preparation

that He has made for us to enjoy, but we can know it only by saying to Him, *"Come ... Let us"*!

LOVING TOGETHER: There will I give you my love.

In the midst of all this scene she was discovering how true her earlier words had been: *"He is altogether lovely,"*[16] but it would have been sad if, through her own neglect, she had never experienced that HE IS ALTOGETHER LOVING!

"There" – not just anywhere, but *"There"*: they were together in the only place where affection and action could be combined in blissful harmony. It was like David saying to them through Psalm 133:3, *"There the LORD commanded the blessing."* Now she knew that the answer to *"Where?"* was *"There,"* and there was no hint of force. Everything was by her permission, yet where did it all start? It was away back in chapter 1 for, if she ever was going to say, *"Let us"*, she must firstly have to say, *"Let him."* These were her first words and the others are among her last. It's also true, if she ever wanted to say, *"Let us go forth"* she firstly had to say, *"I sat down."* If she was ever going to say, *"At our gates are pleasant fruits,"* she firstly had to say, *"His fruit was sweet to my taste."* What she gained in her former experience now pours out in her present expressions.

Firstly, his impressions: finally, her expressions! Putting chapter 2:3 beside chapter 7:8 will let us capture the secret. It was only because she was able to say before, *"Like an apple tree among the trees of the wood, so is my beloved among the sons"* that he was able, afterward, to say, *"The fragrance of your breath like apples."* It's all a matter of first things first, whether this be in safeguarding our first love for Christ or the first principles we have learned both of Him and for Him. All her senses being for him led to all her faculties being for him: her walk, her desires, her vision and, now, her sense of smell. Sharing a common sense of smell meant that they also would be united in their sense of taste. If it were suitable for him, it would be suitable for her. If it were unsuitable for him, it would be unsuitable for her. What a principle for the Christian to live by in the company of our Beloved! If only we were so entirely occupied with absorbing the glories of Christ the loveliest Man of all!

> Ever *"altogether lovely"*, ever, all, most sweet;
> Richest fragrance ever rising round His feet.
> Contemplating every aspect, every feature fair,
> Find we precious, peerless beauty everywhere.

If we are going to know anything of the bride's experience, individually or collectively, we will need to hear the Lord's call as clearly as she heard the words – *"Return, return ... Return, return."* He has something to say to us. He knows that we love Him, but perhaps He is waiting for our actions to confirm our affections. How satisfying it will be when we meet Him and see the marks of Calvary, if He will welcome us, and we welcome Him, with the simultaneous and mutual greeting on our lips – "How beautiful are your feet!"

SANDALED FEET
I have taken off my robe, how can I put it on again?"
I have washed my feet, how can I defile them? (Song 5:3)
Without a robe or sandals on her feet,
Her day is spent, and her whole self reclines:
Unready now, and unprepared to meet,
The voice of the beloved she declines. (Song 5:2)

He stood and knocked, unmoved she stayed alone,
Till he put in his hand, and being moved (Song 5:4)
She rose, forsook the comfort she had known,
And outward went to find the one she loved.

Unseen by us, alas, to us unknown,
Rider of the clouds, Sov'reign of the throne, (Deut.33:26)
Stepped down to grace a far off dusty street,
Where cobbler waits to give Him sandaled feet.

In effortless dominion of the skies
He walked above the circle of the heav'n; (Job 22:14)
Yet now, in shoes that no man e'er unties,
Descends to wear what fallen man has giv'n.

Until a soldier did what none had done:
Untied or snapped each lace and tossed aside
The sandals worn by God's beloved Son,
Then nailed those feet, and watched Him till He died.

And now He comes to knock, to speak and move
The hearts of those whom He has brought to God.
O, may He never see that lack of love
Finds us unmoved, and with our feet unshod! (Eph.6:15)

10

SEALS

"Set me as a seal upon your heart,
as a seal upon your arm,
for love is strong as death,
jealousy is fierce as the grave.
Its flashes are flashes of fire,
the very flame of the LORD."
(Song of Songs 8:6 ESV)

* * *

The great beauty of the Song is that it begins with him on her heart, and ends with her on his. Those famous words, "My beloved is to me" saw him like "A bundle of myrrh" at the centre of her affections. Now she knows what she is to him, and wants to be at the centre of his. As though tired of earlier insecurity, she wants to be "set" there, and knows it is his work, not hers. She also knows the value of being on his heart and on his arm, that she will be the object of his love and of his strength. We thought earlier, in chapter 5, about how the people of Israel could have recognised priestly thoughts in the

Song, and this is particularly true here for two reasons.

Long before they had a king, their high priests, beginning with Aaron, were identified with the engraving of a signet in stones that united heart and shoulders.[1] We may think that these were two very different parts of his body, but God had the loveliest way of linking them together by means of *"a lace of blue."*[2] By connecting them so visibly, God gave the assurance of the strength of His affections and the affections of His strength, and we can safely assume that it was this combination the bride was looking for in her king.

Set me ...

The bride's longings had matured and changed from her list in chapters 1 and 2 where she had focused on "Kiss me ... Draw me ... Tell me .. brought me ... sustain me ... refresh me ... and embraces me." Now her heart and mind were centred on "Set me" with the thought being attached to the Hebrew word *sīm*, which conveys her desire to be committed, purposed, and appointed. Eliphaz used it when he told Job, *"But as for me, I would seek God, and to God I would **commit** my cause."*[3] It was applied to Daniel when he ***"purposed** in his heart"*[4] not to eat the king's meat. And God used it by promising *"Moreover I will **appoint** a place for My people Israel"*[5] and by giving them *"the place ... which the LORD your God chooses to **set** his name there."*[6] If only God's people had followed the example of the bride by wanting to be set where He wanted to set them. He had appointed them, but they lacked a true sense of purpose and steadfast commitment to the 'What?' and 'Where?' of His appointment. Could the same be said of us?

*Appointed

Paul was delighted to be listed among those whom God had *"set,"* for He had assured him, *"I have set you as a light to the Gentiles."*[7] His word *tithēmi* for "set" was like a New Testament echo of the bride's Old Testament word, *sīm*, for it bears similar translation as purpose, commit, and appoint. Like those who heard him preach in Antioch, we live in the joy of having been *"appointed to eternal life."*[8] Not only are we appointed to it, we also are appointed to what to do with it. Jesus made this clear when He said, *"You did not choose Me, but I chose you and appointed you that you should go and bear fruit"*[9] He made it into a kind of double appointment, and Paul turned it into a triple in 2 Corinthians 10:13,14, when he clarified how each of us can do this. *"We, however, will not boast beyond measure, but within the limits of the sphere which God appointed us – a sphere which especially includes you. For we are not overextending ourselves (as though our authority did not extend to you), for it was to you that we came with the gospel of Christ."* We will never fill the extent of the apostle's ministry, but we can emulate his contentment.

God has called each one of us to fulfil our ministry,[10] and He wants us to learn that our own proper sense of fulfilment lies in fulfilling His. He has set the sphere and the limits for His glory and our good, and this helps us to set ourselves according to His appointment, and not according to our own fancy. We work within our limitations inside His limits, restricted only by the former and never by the latter! The world may have Médecins Sans Frontières, but God doesn't have serviteurs sans frontières – servants without borders.

*Purposed

By their lack of trust, Israel seriously misjudged the steadfastness of God who, in the nation's most troubled times, assured them: *"The LORD of hosts has sworn, saying, "Surely, as I have thought, so it shall come to pass, and as I have purposed, so it shall stand ... For the LORD of hosts has purposed, and who will annul it? His hand is stretched out, and who will turn it back?"*[11] How then could His purpose ever be doubted? And why would their own sense of purpose not come into alignment with His own?

We may well ask ourselves the same questions. Greater than His purpose to save Israel from Babylon, Assyria and Philistia, is *"the eternal purpose which He accomplished in Christ Jesus our Lord."*[12] Through it, He saves us from sin and from the on-going battle with the world, the flesh, and the devil, so how can we choose to withhold the pledge that asks Him to set us as a seal upon His heart? The question should burn deeply into our hearts. Even more so when we note when it was that He chose to save us and call us to Himself. Not at the critical moment when His Holy Spirit brought us under conviction of sin or to the point of repentance, *"but according to His own purpose and grace which was given us in Christ Jesus before time began."*[13]

How infinitely grand is the eternal purpose from the eternal God, that He should want to give us eternal salvation! His "purpose" is His *prothesin*, which comes from *protithemai*, which means to set forth. Once more, we are being reminded what He has "set" for our sake, *"And we know that all things work together for good to those who love God, to those who are the called according to His purpose."*[14] In response, we set ourselves to fulfil His calling, by making His purpose ours.

Lord Jesus, 'tis my purpose
To serve Thee to the end;
Oh, give me grace to follow,
My Master and my Friend.
(J.E. Bode)

*Committed

As part of His purpose and our calling, God has entrusted us with an unequalled stewardship for He *"has committed to us the word of reconciliation."*[15] Yet again, He draws on the word *tithēmi* to emphasise that He has intentionally set it before us. Whether by personal conversation, by one-on-one communication, or by public preaching, our mission is the same: *"The things you have heard from me among many witnesses, commit these to faithful men who will be able to teach others also."*[16] Yet again, it's our friend *paratithēmi* asking us, as He did with Paul, to set before others what God had set before him, and committing them to the same commitment.

He has enlisted us as His messengers with His message, or as Paul wrote, *"We are ambassadors for Christ, as though God were pleading through us."*[17] Paul's reaction was, *"I am set for the defence of the gospel."*[18] By this, he meant he was "set" in such a way that he was fully stretched out to do it. This is so evident from his comment in 2 Corinthians 12:15, *"And I will very gladly spend and be spent for your souls."* He was outstretched, but never overstretched, as we learned from the way he accepted his God-appointed sphere of service. Are we ready to face the cost of such commitment and prove, not only that we are willing to be set, but also willing to be stretched?

Go, labour on, spend and be spent;
Thy joy to do the Father's will.
It is the way the Master went;
Should not the servant tread it still?
(Horatius Bonar)

... as a seal

The bride's appeal was timely, and she probably was well aware she had to be "set" before she could be "a seal." Kings sometimes wore a seal in the form of an engraved ring, but she anticipated Solomon's being worn around his neck, suspended between his shoulders, as if lying on his heart to fulfil the image of affection and power. God's people were no strangers to monarchs' use of seals, and also to the thought of God's desire to *"Bind up the testimony, [and] seal the law among [His] disciples."*[19] This is as God expects it to be, and still does.

We see this from how the Lord took Isaiah's words in chapter 8:18 and applied them to all those who belong to Him in Hebrews 2:13: *"Here am I and the children whom God has given Me."* In harmony with His perfect will for us, the Holy Spirit takes the riches of the New Covenant and promises in Hebrews 10:16, *"I will put [didomi] My laws into their hearts, and in their minds I will write them."* This in itself, is a lovely demonstration of combined affection and power for the word "put" means He will "set," as in Revelation 3:8, *"I have set [didomi] before you an open door."* It also makes Him the engraver, as He inscribes the laws of the gospel and God's will for service in our minds.

It's important to remember that the character of the divine seal always acts in full agreement with divine attributes. They always work together, and never independently. By this we mean, for instance, that God's power never contradicts His wisdom, nor does His justice act at the expense of His holiness. He is powerful in His wisdom, and wise in His power; just in His holiness, and holy in His justice. Bearing this in mind, the nature of His seal is found in His affection, His authority, and in His approval. One is never given without the other, as we see in the life of the Lord Jesus, and *"God the Father has set His seal on Him.*[20]

When the bride made her request known to her beloved, she would have known that she was now the object of his affection, authority, approval, and identity, and our Beloved calls us in our bridal relationship with Him to be equally real in our expectations of Him. Will He, for example, approve of something He doesn't love? Or will He approve of anything He doesn't authorise? Perhaps, we can sum up His seal in the following ways, so that we don't misunderstand His integrity or be misled by our own, sometimes, contradictory standards. At all times, all four aspects are interwoven.

- His affection will not be granted independently of His approval;
- His approbation cannot be given at the expense of His affection;
- His authorisation will not be given without His affection;
- He will not have a seal of affection for anything He doesn't love;
- He won't give His seal of approval for whatever isn't His will;
- He cannot give His authority for something He doesn't approve;
- He will not honour something that does not honour His Name.

Like the bride, when each of us asks the Saviour to "Set me," our best guideline is prayerfully to be assured that our appointment, steadfast commitment, and sense of purpose are according to His. Well might we borrow the conversation between Jehu and Jehonadab in 2 Kings 10:15, 16. *"Is your heart right, as my heart is toward your heart?"* and Jehonadab answered, *"It is."* Jehu said, *"If it is, give me your hand."* So he gave him his *hand, and he took him up into the chariot. Then he said, "Come with me, and see my zeal for the LORD."* With mutual zeal, these men purged out the evil *"according to the word of the LORD."*

It may be that zeal is thought to be good enough evidence for the seal of divine approval to be given, and it was for these two men, but it's not always the case. Paul knew, in spite of his longing for Jews to be saved, that they had *"a zeal for God, but not according to knowledge."*[21] They were just the opposite of Jehu and Jehonadab for their zeal was not "according to the word of the Lord." By contrast, Paul also knew that Epaphras had such a genuine zeal for those in Colossae, Laodicea and Hierapolis that he agonised in prayer for them. Without the slightest doubt, he had Paul's threefold seal, and the Lord's too, since he was *"a faithful minister of Christ."*[22] What a commendation! Timothy also had the same stamp on him, since Paul urged him to be *"a good minister of Jesus Christ, nourished in the words of faith and of the good doctrine."*[23]

Whatever our work is for Him, we need the seal of His affection, authority, and approval, all of which belong to and depend upon having the seal of His identity etched on our hearts and on our service. For this to be a reality, Paul's mandate in Colossians 3:17 must become ours: *"And whatever you do in word or deed, do all in the name of our Lord Jesus Christ, giving thanks to God the Father through Him."* For the honour of his Name, we can have His help in answering whatever questions may arise.

- Do you sense God's seal on what you are doing in youth work?
- Brother and sister, is it evident in the ministry God has given you?
- Elder, is the nature of His fourfold seal seen in your leadership?

The right seal in the wrong place

God expects no less, and this is consistent with expectations He had in earlier days. Go back to the time of Eli in 1 Samuel 2:27-30. Think of him, as high priest wearing holy garments and bearing the names of God's people engraved on his breastplate and shoulder stones. Like Aaron before him, he was called to be what he wore, yet he compromised the holiness of God and the signet of His people by tolerating his sons' sinful behaviour at the altar. The seriousness of this seems to be emphasised in verse 300 where God told Eli that he had honoured *"his sons more than Me, to make yourselves fat with the best of all the offerings of Israel My people."* The word for "yourselves" is plural, in Hebrew meaning more than two, and God's disapproval fell on all three, along with the double-edged promise, *"Those who honour Me I will honour."*

The first use of the word "signet" in Genesis 38:18, is also the first example of the right "seal" being in the wrong place. Judah removed it from its place of security around his neck and put it into the hands of Tamar whose illegitimate child she was expecting. Three months later, she produced *"the signet and cord, and staff"*[24] to prove the identity of the father. Being the book of bringing fallen man back to God, this is only one of the wrongs in Genesis that God overcame, and we find Judah as a tribe given prominence to *"break camp first"*[25] and lead His people through the wilderness. We also find Tamar's name linked with the bride in the Song when her stature is described as being like a "palm tree" [Hebrew *l^etamar*], yet greater stature is granted to her in Matthew 1:3, sealed forever in the genealogy that led to Jesus being born from the tribe of Judah.[26]

The right seal in the right place

Unlike its first use in Scripture, the last reference to a signet in the Old Testament gives God's affection, authority, and approval being identified with a man called Zerubbabel in the closing words of Haggai's short prophecy: *"Speak to Zerubbabel, governor of Judah, saying: 'I will shake heaven and earth. I will overthrow the throne of kingdoms ... 'In that day,' says the LORD of hosts, 'I will take you, Zerubbabel My servant, the son of Shealtiel,' says the LORD,' and will make you like a signet ring; for I have chosen you,' says the LORD of hosts."*[27]

To understand why God marked him out in this way, we need to go back to the book of Ezra to see God's evaluation of him:

- In chapter 2:2, 64-65, a spiritual leader followed by 49,897;
- In chapter 3, a spiritual builder of the altar and the temple (vv.2,8); securing a spiritual relationship in the morning and evening lambs (v.3); ensuring the right approach in worship burnt offerings and the Feasts (vv.4,5); laying the temple's foundation and the foundation of fellowship (vv.10-13);
- In chapter 4:1-3, a spiritual defender resisting the enemy. Chapter 4 opens on a high – i.e. knowing when to say 'No' to the enemy, which is one proof of discipleship; and it closes on a low, the cessation of the work;
- In chapter 5:1,2 setting an example for resuming and finishing the work.

Here was a man of God, so much under the effects of the Word of God and its inspiration that his own sense of being compelled could almost be described as inspired. It was as if he inhaled what God exhaled, so that he lived and breathed the will of God. In Zerubbabel's day, the people of God had lost their sense of being moved, and no wonder for there can be no real motivation when the enjoyment of inspiration has been lost. Their impetus for spiritual recovery had evaporated, and the urging of a foreign king, Cyrus, led them to sense that God was moving their spirits, too.[28]

There is no limit to what He can do through those that He moves. Into this vacuum of a down-tools' mentality stepped two God-appointed men, Haggai and Zechariah, with ministry that was the source of inspiration and motivation. God breathed it out and the people, including Joshua and Zerubbabel, breathed it in. *"The LORD stirred the spirit"* and everyone *"came and worked."*[29] If they had been asked why they went back to work, their answers could have been different depending upon which prophet they had heard. One may have said, "Oh, I heard Haggai and he was tough. His message was, *"Consider ... build ... work."*[30] Another may have said, "Oh, I heard Zechariah and he was tender. He didn't urge us to build; his message was, *'Behold, the Man,'*[31] and this appeal made me want to work."

In the midst of it all, Zerubbabel became a marked man, with marks of Christ-likeness made by God.

- A builder (Hag.1:1,2; cf. Matt.16:18);
- An example of obedience (Hag.1:12; cf. 1 Pet.2:21);
- God calls him, *"My servant"* (Hag.2:23; cf. Is.53:10-12);
- Filled with the Spirit (Zech.4:6; cf. Matt.12:18);
- A beginner and finisher (Zech.4:9; cf. Lk.4:1);
- A plumbline in his hand (Zech.4:10; cf. Heb.12:2);
- A son of oil (Zech.4:14; cf. Lk.4:16-20, Jn 3:11).

He was a lovely foreshadowing of the Saviour, but we note the way that

God reached for him: "I will shake ... I will take ... I will make." Although the first of these is very different from the other two, all three show the omnipotence of God. He will rid Israel of all hostile powers that come against her, both in Zerubbabel's day and in the future when at last they will come to Christ as their Messiah, and as the "Desire of All Nations."[32] The second and third show His divine power demonstrated in taking and making Zerubbabel His signet. This implies that its impress would grant divine approval on his word, his walk, and on his work? At the time of bearing the honour of the One he honoured, he valued being as near to God as His royal seal. This marked him out as being different from his predecessors:

- Judah: Gave his signet to Tamar in the lust of the flesh in Genesis 38 – **DEVALUED**;
- Jehoiachin: Lost the right to be God's seal and was rejected by God for his evil in Jeremiah 22:24-26 – **DISCARDED**;
- The bride: Accepted as a seal by her beloved in the Song – **DEVOTION**;
- Zerubbabel: Chosen as a seal by God – **DELIGHT**.

I will make you

Before a seal can be formed, some bits have to be cut away. If unwanted bits remain, it prevents the seal being made and the king's image would be impossible. So the bride's lethargy and apathy had to go. It's the same with us, but each of us needs to ask, 'What has to go?" There needs to be a mark made by God before we can make a mark for God, and we often give thanks for those who do. Do you wonder why you are not making a mark for Him? He needs to make an impact on you before He can make an impact through you. You need to be impressionable before you can make an impression!

Many things in life are complete in themselves, but even more complete when complemented with something else. The simple reason is, they are made for each other: such as, a lock and key, a pen and paper, a mortise and tenon joint, a husband and wife. It's also true of a signet and wax. Are you there for the taking? If not, tell Him right now. Are you there for the making? If so, tell Him right now. Zerubbabel name means 'begotten in Babylon.' You are begotten of God, so you should be! Whatever stage you are at, will you allow Him to shake you, then take you and make you? Bow before Him where you are and say, "Christ of the lowly heart, Christ of the nail-pierced hand, *set me as a seal upon Your heart, as a seal upon your arm."* I am ready – *"my heart is like wax."*[33]

OH! TO BE LIKE THEE

Oh! to be like Thee, blessed Redeemer,
This is my constant longing and prayer;
Gladly I'll forfeit all of earth's treasures,
Jesus, Thy perfect likeness to wear.

Oh! to be like Thee, oh! to be like Thee,
Blessed Redeemer, pure as Thou art;
Come in Thy sweetness, come in Thy fullness;
Stamp Thine own image deep on my heart.

Oh! to be like Thee, full of compassion,
Loving, forgiving, tender and kind,
Helping the helpless, cheering the fainting,
Seeking the wand'ring sinner to find.

Oh! to be like Thee, lowly in spirit,
Holy and harmless, patient and brave;
Meekly enduring cruel reproaches,

Willing to suffer, others to save.

Oh! to be like Thee, Lord, I am coming,
Now to receive th' anointing divine;
All that I am and have I am bringing,
Lord, from this moment all shall be Thine.

Oh! to be like Thee, while I am pleading,
Pour out Thy Spirit, fill with Thy love,
Make me a temple meet for Thy dwelling,
Fit me for life and Heaven above.
(Thomas O. Chisolm)

11

JEHOVAH'S NAMES

"Set me as a seal upon your heart,
As a seal upon your arm;
For love is as strong as death,
Jealousy as cruel as the grave;
Its flames are flames of fire,
A most vehement flame."
(Song of Songs 8:6)

* * *

Does the name of God appear in the Song of songs? It is commonly believed that the answer is, 'No.' According to fairly popular belief, there are two books in our Bible that do not contain the word "God" - the story of Esther and the Song. But is it true? Again, the answer is, 'No', and this is supported by at least five English versions.[1] Their reason for this is found in chapter 8:6 – *"Set me as a seal upon your heart, as a seal upon your arm, for love is as strong as death, jealousy is fierce as the grave. Its flashes are flashes of fire, the very flame of the LORD."* Of these five versions, four use the word

"LORD," and the ASV says, "Jehovah," while others refer to a mighty or most vehement flame. The reason for this is the Hebrew word *shalhebet-yah*, which combines the flame with the name of Jehovah to convey its intensity, and other portions of Scripture refer to the fire of God in association with both judgment and worship.[2]

How fitting it is that, in the best of all songs, His name is introduced to emphasise the strongest and securest love. Verse 7 (ESV) goes on to say, *"Many waters cannot quench love, neither can floods drown it. If a man offered for love all the wealth of his house, he would be utterly despised."* It can't be extinguished, since it is so distinguished; and it can't be sold off at any price, since infinite love has an infinite cost! The Shulamite had reached her highest appreciation of kingly love. If only Israel, as God's people, had done the same! God had bought them with His love. They were *"The redeemed of the LORD,"*[3] and so are we through infinite grace shown at the infinite cost of the blood of His Son. He paid a debt He did not owe, and we owed a debt we could not pay!

My beloved – his virtues

If we consider the virtues of the bridegroom we must also see how his words and behaviour interact with the different words and behaviour of his bride. In this we will see a sequence of virtues that we can readily identify with the Lord Jesus Christ, and with His God and Father. Around its setting in the library of Old Testament writings, the language and imagery are regularly confirmed as God conveying His relationship with Israel, and this encourages us to see the name of Jehovah throughout the Song, just as it is throughout Scripture.

Isaiah linked His name for His people to sing of their *"Beloved regarding His vineyard ... For the vineyard of the LORD of hosts is the house of Israel."*[4]

Jeremiah did likewise: *"Thus says the LORD, I remember you, the kindness of your youth, the love of your betrothal."*[5] And Hosea added, *"The word of the LORD that came to Hosea ... Then she will say, I will go and return to my first husband, for then it was better for me than now."*[6] Right from the beginning of their bridal bond with Him, the One who formed the bond kept the bond, and always assured them of His Jehovah name. By seeing how these portions consistently show that Israel's Beloved is Jehovah, we can go through the Song to discover the manifestations of the Jehovah Names.

Since they are equally applicable to our Lord Jesus Christ, we can take each aspect of our 'Interpretations of the Song' and see 'My Beloved – His virtues' not only in connection with the Father, but also for us in His Son. As Christians, we should know how to recognise and emphasise the glories of His Jehovah-Names, and how they are seen in our Saviour.

Jehovah-Ropheka: Your name is ointment poured forth - 1:3

To understand this imagery, as we thought earlier, all we have to do is imagine the effects of this happening: its value, its aroma, its ability to permeate, while being unseen, but not unfelt. This will lead into thoughts of Him *"whom having not seen you love."*[7]

In Hebrew, the word for ointment is *shemen* which comes from the word *shāman* to speak of riches, being fruitful or shining in ways that cause us to think of Christlike features like grace, forgiveness, comfort, compassion, beauty and strength. Like the bride, we also recognise that in our Beloved's features are many, even though the fragrance is one. For her, it was the same. The word *"ointments"* is plural, while *"fragrance"* is singular.

The word *"good"* in 1:3 is identical to the word *"better"* in verse 2 – *"your love is better than wine"* – and this is a lovely way of pointing us to all the better things that the letter to the Hebrews shows we have in Christ. The real beauty of the Song is, she describes the bridegroom's ointments in chapter 1:3 as the graces of his life, and he describes her ointments in chapter 4:10 as the graces of her life. Although the New King James Version speaks of *"perfumes,"* it is from the same word, *shemen*. We may wonder how can we possess such graces in our Christian lives, and we learn from her that it is by absorbing them from our Beloved! It's as if we take in what He pours out, so that we can show patience, meekness, sympathy, etc., as if we had inner vials of each.

In Ecclesiastes 7:1, Solomon tells us that *"a good name is better than precious ointment,"* then shortly afterwards in chapter 10:1 he adds, *"Dead flies putrefy the perfumer's ointment, and cause it to give off a foul odour."* He knew that putrefying flesh produces stench instead of sweetness. How easily the dead flies of our flesh do that in our lives too! Do you have any, such as impatience, intolerance, aggression, pride, grudges, a critical spirit? The story is told of an argumentative woman passenger leaving a bus, and the driver said to her, "You have left something behind, lady." As she turned to look back, he added, "A bad impression." How true it is, that, according to our temperament, we either emit the scent of ointment or the stench of dead flies. We can't have both! The bride never said that her beloved had a name like ammonia or liniment. There was no pungent character or bad reputation. Likewise, we cannot say this of our precious Saviour, but is He saying it about us? How much we need to exercise our senses, as Hebrews 5:14 demands!

After the redemption of Exodus 12, Jehovah-Ropheka (Jehovah the Healer) is the first to be mentioned when God told His people in chapter

15:26, *"I am the LORD who heals you."* Rather significantly, it is the first to be inferred in the Song where the bride's physical separation and emotional upheavals were representative of Israel's spiritual condition. The remedy lay in enjoying love's relationship with Jehovah-Ropheka who was available to them in three very important ways, and you will see how closely each was related to His Jehovah name:

- **PHYSICALLY** - *Who heals all your diseases* (Psalm 103:3). *Bless the LORD ...*
- **EMOTIONALLY** - *He heals the brokenhearted* (Psalm 147:3). *The LORD...*
- **SPIRITUALLY** - *He has torn, but He will heal us* (Hosea 6:1). *Return to the LORD.*

There was never any need for the people of Israel to be bereft of help, though Jeremiah faced up to the reality of their poor spiritual condition when he asked, *"Is there no balm in Gilead, is there no physician there? Why then is there no recovery for the health of the daughter of my people?"*[8] The answer was simple: they had no desire to cry out to Jehovah-Ropheka as Jeremiah did, *"Heal me, O LORD, and I shall be healed; save me, and I shall be saved, for You are my praise."*[9] As for our own with the Saviour, they can be remedied only by the Lord our Healer, and we can turn to Him as dependently as Israel could.

Jehovah-Ro'ī: Where you feed your flock, where you make it rest at noon - 1:7

This is a picture of a typically caring, feeding, leading shepherd, and a lovely picture of Jehovah-Ro'ī, the LORD-the Shepherd, as we find captured in Psalm 23. As we said when thinking about this in 'Men God Moved – Grace in first Peter' - we are accustomed to saying, "The LORD is my Shepherd," yet the Hebrew word *rā'āh* is a verb and means "The LORD shepherds me" or "The LORD is shepherding me." As far as David was concerned, it wasn't only that the LORD was His shepherd, but that He was actively shepherding him. In His wonderful grace to Israel, He gave the lamb for their Passover deliverance, and then the Shepherd stepped in to lead them out from the place of bondage. The scene is relived in Psalm 78:52-55:

> "He made His own people go forth like sheep, and guided them in the wilderness like a flock; and He led them on safely, so that they did not fear; but the sea overwhelmed their enemies. And He brought them to His holy border, this mountain which His right hand had acquired. He also drove out the nations before them, allotted them an inheritance by survey, and made the tribes of Israel dwell in their tents."

What a magnificent summary this is! Phrase after phrase builds a cumulative sense of the pastoral and powerful nature of Jehovah. He delivers, He directs, He defends, by the fulness of his heart and the firmness of His hands. In His affection for them, He also promised in Ezekiel 34:13-15:

> "'I will bring them out from the peoples and gather them from the countries, and will bring them to their own land; I will feed them

on the mountains of Israel, in the valleys and in all the inhabited places of the country. I will feed them in good pasture, and their fold shall be on the high mountains of Israel. There they shall lie down in a good fold and feed in rich pasture on the mountains of Israel. I will feed My flock, and I will make them lie down," says the LORD God.'"

The Song shows that shepherd work is day and night,[10] and only God, Jehovah-Roʻī , could say with such meaning to His people, *"He who keeps Israel shall neither slumber nor sleep. The LORD is your keeper, the LORD is your shade at your right hand. The sun shall not strike you by day, nor the moon by night."*[11]

Do shepherds in your church know where their sheep are? Do they know how they are? Ezekiel spoke about sheep that were diseased, sick, broken, driven away and lost. They needed help: strengthening, healing, binding up, gathering in and keeping safe, but the so-called shepherds didn't care. How unlike the great Jehovah-Roʻī they were! To this day, God uses men to fill the office of shepherds in the care of His people, but does this mean that sisters have no pastoral role to fill? One of the great aspects of truth related to the church, which is the body of Christ, is that there is *"neither male nor female"*[12] in it. All believers are *"members"*[13] of it and, as such, possess spiritual gifts that can be equally used in the service of God. This means that God's women can be similarly gifted to men, similarly used, and similarly moved by Him to fulfil certain roles, even though their sphere may be different. Elders should fulfil their shepherding work in the churches, but there is no shortage of opportunities for sisters to have a meaningful ministry of shepherd care toward others.

Jehovah-Tsidkenu: Behold, you are fair, my love! - 1:15. Behold, thou art fair, my beloved - 1:16 RV.

This is mutual appreciation and attraction, yet earlier in chapter 1:5 she had said, *"I am dark"* – which was how she saw herself; *"but lovely"* – that is, what she was to him. Thankfully, by the time she reached chapter 8:10 she had reached a completely different outlook, for then she would be ready to think of what she had become *"in his eyes."* However, being in her present mindset, she added, *"Do not look upon me, because I am dark,"* and, as we will see later, he certainly fulfilled her request. Self-consciousness and inferiority complex can hinder spiritual progress, whether it belongs to thinking we are inadequate in ourselves or not good enough in what we do.

For the bride, both of these were issues for she was equally concerned that her brothers had made her the keeper of the vineyards, but her own vineyard she had not kept. There may be times when we are tempted into thinking negatively of ourselves, but we should rest in this, that neither thoughts of inferiority or superiority should spoil the minds of those who are in Christ. There may also be times when we wrestle with what others may insist we should be doing. This can lead to real conflict of interests, and, as it did with this young Shulamite, make you neglect what God wants you to do. Better to focus on what He has made your own than to be distracted, because others "made me." What matters is pleasing God, even when it means disappointing others!

Human nature can get in the way of spiritual perception, and God overcame this by seeing all twelve tribes of His people represented in the twelve loaves of the showbread in the holy place of the tabernacle. This allowed Him, through the character of the bread, to say that *"He has not observed iniquity in Jacob, nor has He seen wickedness in Israel."*[14] Instead,

He viewed the righteousness they had before Him, because, as their Beloved, He was their Jehovah-Tsidkēnū, the LORD-our righteousness. The day will come when, in the presence of the Man whose name is the Branch, *"Israel will dwell safely; now this is His name by which He shall be called: "The LORD-OUR RIGHTEOUSNESS."*[15] In that day, *"the ransomed of the LORD shall return, and come to Zion with singing."*[16]

Meanwhile, believers in the Lord Jesus Christ are *"accepted in the Beloved"*[17] and, having been *"made righteous"*[18] in Him, we have come to know the Lord Jesus as Jehovah-Tsidkēnū, the LORD-our Righteousness. Only in Him can each believer say:

> I once was a stranger to grace and to God
> I knew not my danger and felt not my load.
> Though friends spoke in rapture of Christ on the tree,
> Jehovah-Tsidkenu was nothing to me.
>
> My terrors all vanished before the sweet name;
> My guilty fears banished, with boldness I came
> To drink at the fountain, life giving and free—
> Jehovah Tsidkenu is all things to me.
> (Robert Murray McCheyne)

Only because we are in Him, can He say, *"You are all fair, My love; and there is no spot in you."*[19] How could Israel miss this precious reminder of the lamb that was without blemish, even though they knew nothing of the One to whom it pointed and through whom they also will be made perfect in a day to come? Christ has taken us out of our natural sinful state and has brought us into the perfection of the Lamb.[20] Because of this, we can sing:

Let us with joy adopt the strain
We hope to sing for ever there –
"Worthy the Lamb for sinners slain,
Worthy alone the crown to wear!"
Without one thought that's good to plead,
Oh, what could shield us from despair,
But this – though we are vile indeed,
The Lord our righteousness is there?
(A. Rutherford)

Jehovah-Jireh: His fruit … His banqueting house - 2:3,4

When Solomon led the Shulamite forward, it was with the promise of full preparation and provision, and it gives a glimpse of how God did this for Israel when, having entered Canaan, *"they ate of the fruit of the land of Canaan that year."*[21] They had a Beloved who revealed Himself as Jehovah-Jireh, the LORD will provide, and so do we, yet there are times when we eat the fruit of the land and other times when we don't. There are times when heaven is opened and our hands are not! Even when He says "No", He is providing! His denials are not deprivations, but part of His supply.[22] He is the One who invites us to know more about *"the fulness of Christ."*[23] A banquet is set before us, but will we be satisfied by such a rich banquet from Jehovah-Jireh or will we be content with our own meagre appetite for sandwiches? It was on the way to Moriah that God introduced Himself to Abraham as Jehovah-Jireh, and it was in that place of Moriah, the same area as Calvary, that we were introduced to our Jehovah-Jireh who fully provided for us on the cross.

Jehovah-Nissi: And his banner over me was love - 2:4

It was as if her beloved had hoisted a banner on a conspicuous standard with the word 'LOVE' emblazoned on it. It was because of God's love that Israel was chosen, and in her encampment she was accustomed to banners and standards.[24] Her tribes also knew that their word *diglō* for *"banner"* or *"standard"* had the special meaning of being conspicuous. She also knew that above them floated the greatest banner of all, Jehovah-Nissī: the LORD is my Banner. Being under the banner of Love's victory always follows being under the banner of Love's protection. It is impossible to be inconspicuous or defeated there!

The bride was under the shadow and under the banner. Israel was under the blood, under the cloud, and under the Law. What are we under? We are under grace, under the Lordship of our Saviour, and we have protection and triumph too. There is a mighty defence under His blood that the enemy cannot break through. There is no such word in His vocabulary as 'defeat,' and no possibility of it unless we are not living under His banner. There is no turmoil there for *"You have given a banner to those who fear You, that it may be displayed because of the truth."*[25] In the days of the tabernacle encampment *"every man* [was] *by his own standard,"*[26] and how can there be any less a sense of personal commitment by those who belong to our Lord Jesus Christ?

Jehovah-Shalom

The thought of peace is expressed in three different ways in the Song:

- **IMAGERY:** *"You have dove's eyes"* (1:15);
- **CONDITIONS:** *"The winter is past, the rain is over and gone"* (2:11);

· **COMMUNION:** *"I became in his eyes as one who found peace"* (8:10).

This is the threefold blessing of walking with Jehovah-Shalom, Jehovah our Peace. There is no cold stare in the way we look at others, no frosted ground of winter, and no cooling off or barrenness in the presence of the LORD our Peace. He wants communion with us, and grants it as we *"let the peace of Christ rule in your hearts."*[27] After much waywardness, the day will come when Israel *"shall see eye to eye when the LORD brings back Zion."*[28] And, then, they will enjoy a thousand years of peace in the presence of the One who, right now, is our Jehovah-Shalom, having *"made peace through the blood of His cross."*[29]

Jehovah-Shammah: When I found the one I love (3:4).

Times of searching and finding, times of departure and return were as real to Israel as they were for the bride. To them, the cloud announced *"Jehovah-Shammah,"* and by revelation through the prophets it was confirmed, *"THE LORD IS THERE."*[30] In every age, finding Him and holding Him in the reality of a close personal relationship, is the surest way of stating this truth with deepest conviction. In the joy of being where He wants us to be with Him belongs the best experience that belongs to telling Him, *"There I will give You my love."*[31] Then, like the woman at the well in John 4:29, we will call others, *"Come, see a Man."*

132

Jehovah-Mekaddishkem: Come with me ... with me - 4:8. Come, my beloved - 7:11-13.

To be apart with him and for him, just to be entirely his, was what the bridegroom wanted for his bride, and it's also what God wanted for Israel. He was Jehovah their Sanctifier (Ex.31:13), setting them apart in holiness for Himself. He wanted them to experience that where there is godliness there is gladness. Israel knew, as many present-day believers do, that this is the Name which imparts very greatest responsibility, for the imparting of His character demands holy living by those who share it. Sadly, Israel treated God's holiness, and the expectation of their own, in a very off-handed manner. Neither of these appealed to them when they were mired in sin and ungodliness, until Isaiah told God, *"We have become like those of old, over whom you never ruled, like those who are not called by your name."*[32] They belonged to Jehovah, yet His name made no sanctifying impression on them.

Well, these things were written for our learning and admonition, and God's message to us in our day is, *"Pursue peace with all people, and holiness, without which no one will see the Lord."*[33] Peter agrees with this and urges us, *"but sanctify Christ as Lord in your hearts."*[34] Living in the blessing of these aspects of sanctification will only be possible when His desire and ours are combined like the bride and bridegroom in the Song. He will say to us, *"Come with Me,"* and we will respond, *"Come, my Beloved."*

Jehovah-Tsebāōth: My beloved is ... chief among ten thousand - 5:10 - distinguished, marked out by a banner. Awesome as an army with banners - 6:4!

He is head of the host, and she is like a bannered host. She has already delighted in the Jehovah-Nissī-like relationship of his banner being over her in chapter 2:4. Now, borrowing from the same root word *dāgal* that gave the noun *we̅diglō*, she uses the verb form to describe him as "Chief" to show how distinguished and outstanding he is. He does exactly the same in chapter 6:4 by using the word *kannidgālōt*, and their similarity proclaims a mutual likeness: he is victorious for her, and she is victorious for him. As far as she is concerned, he is conspicuously hers; and he views her as conspicuously his. It's as if no superlative is great enough for them to use for the other, and he makes it clear that no compliment is too high for him to give her. He is her "Chief," and he responds in chapter 6:4, "*O my love, you are beautiful as Tirzah, lovely as Jerusalem.*" To him, she was like the chief cities in Israel, the combined capitals of north and south, which let her bring her majesty to him as he brought his to her. What tremendous lessons are embedded in this, firstly for Israel, and then for those who belong to Christ and His church!

When Israel gave God His place she was victorious, led in triumph, never defeated. Their God was Jehovah-Tse̅baōth, the LORD of hosts (1 Sam.17:45). To go with Him was to win, and this we discover through our Lord Jesus Christ, the Captain of the LORD's host.[35] We should learn from Deuteronomy 25:17-18 when Amalek smote the tail-end, that being on the fringe of God's people leaves us exposed and vulnerable, rather than always being led "*in triumph in Christ*"[36] and in the all-authority of the LORD of hosts.

When the Master was led from Gethsemane the people of Israel failed to recognise Him as such, even though He said that He could call for more than twelve legions of angels. What a Commander! When He comes to reign, they will see that the Man, Jesus, is after all equal with God[37] and that, as Jehovah the Saviour, He fully displays all the Jehovah names. Meanwhile, we walk with our Beloved and rejoice that He is all of these to those who love Him.

On one occasion Abraham Lincoln and his counsellors had taken an important decision. One of them said, "Well, Mr President, I hope that God is on our side." Lincoln answered, "What I am worried about is, not if God is on our side, but if we are on God's side." May we always be on the side of Jehovah-Tsabaoth, the LORD of hosts.

Jehovah-Jireh
Jehovah-Jireh (Gen.22:14)
God will provide – Oh what a Name
He meets all my needs now:
Today and ever the same.
Riches in glory, all in Christ Jesus:
Jehovah-Jireh, forever mine.

Jehovah-Shalom. (Judg.6:24)
The LORD is peace – Tremendous Name:
His cross my answer,
His blood my only claim.
He said *"Tis finished!"* the work accomplished.
Jehovah-Shalom, I call Him mine.

Jehovah-Rohi. (Ps.23:1)
The LORD, my Shepherd – I'll never lack.

E'en in the valley
He turns the shadow back.
When I need comfort I call that Name divine:
Jehovah-Rohi, and He calls Mine.

Jehovah-Nissi. (Ex.17:15)
The LORD, my banner – His love my might.
Under His shadow
I sit with great delight.
And in His house of wine I'm my Beloved's:
Jehovah-Nissi, and He is mine.

Jehovah-Shammah. (Ezek.48:35)
The LORD is there – Whose Name is Love.
The Omnipresent
On earth, in heaven above;
And when in glory, and His own image share,
Jehovah-Shammah, I'll see Him there.

12

WALKING WITH HIM

"What would you see
in the Shulamite –
As it were
the dance of the two camps?"
(Song of Songs 6:13)

* * *

Who was best to answer this question? The bridegroom's immediate answer shows what he thought of her, but was he the only one to whom the question was directed? Perhaps, not! In the first purpose of the Song, he undoubtedly was, but what about the application of the Song? In the mind of God, as its Inspirer, the purpose went much farther than Solomon had in winning his Shulamite. For long years, another struggle raged with which Solomon's was but little in comparison. Having defiantly insisted on being like other nations by having their own king, God gave His people one in His anger,[1] yet they still failed to be subject to Him, and turmoil reigned even after He took him away in His wrath and put David on the throne. Against that background, the bride's question should have drawn a much-needed response from Israel.

Having been a divided kingdom,[2] they could have seen themselves in the "the dance of the two camps," and been made to think of what God was saying to them as a nation about their relationship with Him. The Targum presents this as the two camps of Israel and Judah. Had they been sensitive to language of the Song, they could have seen certain comments as reflections of themselves, not only as Israel and Judah, but as twelve individual tribes.

*Judah: Praise - 1:4, 12; 3:9, 11; 7:5

References to the king marked out the bride as his partner in the kingly tribe and resident of the kingly city. His father, David, had spoken highly of it in Psalm 48, "*Great is the LORD, and greatly to be praised in the city of our God ... the city of the great King. God is in her palaces, He is known as her refuge.*" The Shulamite enjoyed the thought of being brought into his chambers, of being at his table, and seeing him crowned in his majesty. She was so typical of what they should have been enjoying in the presence of God, their King. Alas, when the King came to His rightful city, they rejected Him, too, and the One who wept at the death of Lazarus wept even more over it, and they completely missed bringing their glory to His feet.

*Issachar: Reward - 6:13, 8:11,12

As if rewarding her dignity, Solomon gave his own name to his bride by calling her, "Shulamite," of which Wycliffe says, "The designation *Shulamite* for the bride is likely derived from the place of Shunem," a place in the region of Issachar.[3] If they thought about this, they may also have thought of the meaning of their own name when she spoke about the payment made to the keepers of the vineyard for their work, and to Solomon. It certainly should have provoked them to think about how rewarding the service of God is for those who are diligent in his vineyard.

*Zebulun: Dwelling - 7:11; 8:13

He had already asked three times that she would "Come away" and "Come with me," and she had only once appealed, *"Let my beloved come to his garden."* 4 But her second call was different: *"Come, my beloved … Let us lodge in the villages."* This went beyond the joy of being together for it meant staying together. From all the past and its unsettled days, they wanted to be settled in complete satisfaction with each other. What a voice to the tribe of Zebulun with their own meaning of "dwelling," as if in an enclosed place! The bride almost echoed this by choosing "the villages" for these also indicate places that are surrounded by walls. If only their desire to dwell with God had mirrored her appeal!

> We are a garden walled around,
> Chosen and made peculiar ground;
> A little spot enclosed by grace
> Out of the world's wide wilderness.
> (Isaac Watts)

When Solomon said, *"I have surely built thee an house to dwell in,"*[5] he used the word *z^{e}bul* for "dwell," knowing it was part of Zebulun's name. The difficulty was that Zebulun didn't always live in the enjoyment of the meaning of his name.

*Reuben: See a son - 3:3; 5:8; 7:12

Can you imagine a bride losing sight of her beloved and having to ask the watchmen of the city, "Have you seen the one I love?" or needing to urge other young women that they should tell him she was lovesick? How different she was from Jonathan who, at the very time Saul's forces searched for David and couldn't find him, *"went to David in the woods and strengthened his hand in God."*[6] Love found the way, and should never need to pass on its message by hearsay! Her failure to see was highlighted by asking what others had "seen." She used the word *rā'āh*, which refers to the gaze or sharp-sightedness of a bird of prey, and linked to the kite. It's also the word that, when combined with *ben*, forms the basis of Reuben's name. Like the bride, and other tribes too, they had taken their eyes off God, and needed help to see Him and to find Him.

In this lesson, God was teaching Reuben and all His people, as He would later say through Jeremiah, *"And you will seek Me and find Me, when you search for Me with all your heart."*[7] The bride learned the hard way that she shouldn't depend on others to see, to find or to tell, and finally found that the secret lay in saying, "Let us see." At last, she put the implications of the word *ra'ah* in the right place! She must see as her beloved sees, and see what he sees, and neither of these was possible when she wasn't with him. It was like this for Reuben and all Israel, too, but the day is coming when their *"Watchmen shall lift up their voices, with their voices they shall sing together; for they shall see [yir'ū – from rā'āh] eye to eye when the LORD brings back Zion."*[8] He will put the *ra'ah* into Reuben in a way it has never been before!

*Simeon: Hearing - 2:8,10,14; 5:2; 8:13

One of the delightful features of the Song is their mutual regard for each other's voice, without which there is no real hearing. Twice she exclaimed, "The voice of my beloved!" and on two occasions he spoke about hers. However, the big difference is, that only he ever said, "Let me hear it!" Full communion needs both, and as Christians we will make no progress without God's voice being heard by us, and our voices being heard by Him. It was the beloved who emphasised his need to hear her, and his phrase comes from the word *shāma*, which is at the heart of the name Simeon. How much they needed to hear the voice of God as their Beloved, and be able to say, "My beloved spoke, and said to me"!

When God spoke again through Hosea, He called for Israel to return and to *"Take words with you ... Say to him, "Take away all iniquity; receive us graciously, for we will offer the sacrifices of our lips."*[9] It was His way of saying, "Let Me hear your voice," and asking them to make these words as valuable as "bullocks" (ASV) would be at His altar. Simeon was among those to whom He spoke, as God emphasised the need to be heard and to hear. It's an unchanging principle for His people, both then and now, that we walk with Him by hearing and being heard. We do not walk by sight, but we do walk by hearing!

*Gad: Overcomer - 3:7,8

The question, "Who is this coming out of the wilderness?" leaves us to conclude that the Shulamite is the passenger, since the word "this," *zo't*, is feminine, and that she is being transported to her king in Jerusalem. She is encircled by sixty valiant men, and safely escorted in their strength and mastery as expert guardsmen. It's as if she is surrounded by a troop who will overcome. When Gad was born, *"Leah said, "A troop comes!" So she called his name Gad."*[10] As he stood beside his father's deathbed with his brothers, his parting words to his son were, *"A troop shall overcome him, but he shall overcome at last."*[11]

*Ephraim: Doubly fruitful - 2:12,13; 7:12,13

Fruitfulness is one of the great indicators that the bridegroom and bride's relationship was to their pleasing, and good signs of fruitfulness were there in the early stages of their friendship, as green figs and tender grapes pointed forward to riper days. Later, they looked together with joyful anticipation on the flourishing vine and blossoming pomegranates. As they did, the bride proclaimed her long-awaited assurance: *"At our gates are pleasant fruits, all manner, new and old, which I have laid up for you, my beloved."* Now it was "our entrance," a place of access to their combined satisfaction and pleasure, so that their going out and in might be a constant reminder of her ever-increasing fruitfulness since earlier days.

The whole scene is one that exudes the fulness of each believer's opportunity to present the hoarded resources we have in Christ. We live in the full assurance *"of the hope which is laid up for you in heaven ... which has come to you ... and is bringing forth fruit, as it is also among you since the day you heard and knew the grace of God in truth."*[12]

*Manasseh: Causing to forget

By the end of the song, there was much to make the beloved rejoice, and much for the bride to forget. Her path to his pleasure had been chequered, yet he graciously helped her to forget the things that were behind. Unlike the ten tribes from Jacob's sons that were named by their mothers, Manasseh had his name given by Joseph, his father, as a testimony that *"God has made me forget all my toil and my father's house."*[13] Jacob's family had much to live down for the way they treated him, yet he forgave them for the anguish they had caused, saying, *"you meant evil against me; but God meant it for good."*[14] That was a remarkable day for Jacob's sons, granted by a rejected brother, but a more miraculous day is coming when *"The Redeemer will come to Zion, and to those who turn from transgression in Jacob."*[15] In that day, He will cause them to forget!

*Benjamin: Son of the right hand - 2:6; 8:3

Just as it could be said of Jacob's love for Benjamin, that *"his life is bound up in the lad's life,"*[16] so the life of the bridegroom in the Song became bound up in the life of his bride. She considered him to be unique *"among the sons"*[17] and he became like a son of the right hand to her, since she thought of his left hand being under her head and his right hand embracing her, both in the times she wanted to forget in chapter 2:6 and in days she always wanted to remember in chapter 8:3.

Asaph's appeal to the "Shepherd of Israel" in Psalm 80 links Joseph in verse 1 with Benjamin in verse 2. Had Jacob allowed Rachel's choice of name to stand, verse 2 would have called him Ben-Oni, son of my sorrow. Later, in verse 15, reference is made to *"The vineyard which Your right hand has planted, and the branch that You made strong for Yourself"* or, as the Hebrew word *ben,* for "branch," means, the son. This would appear to refer to Israel as the vine and vineyard, and also as the "son of man" in verse 17 – *"Let Your hand be upon the man of your right hand, upon the son of man whom You made strong for Yourself."*

The Psalmist's longing is that God will restore His people, and the full answer to his prayer still waits for the appearing of their Messiah. He appeared once as "Man of sorrows" and was rejected by them, but He will come *"with power and great glory"*[18] as the true Son of Man and Son of the right hand. It has been put this way: "He was Benoni, Son of my sorrow; but as Jacob, his father called him subsequently Benjamin, 'son of the right hand'; so Messiah, once "A Man of sorrows" (Is.53:3), was exalted by the right hand of the Father to be Prince and Saviour (Acts 5:31)" (Jamieson, Fausset and Brown).

*Dan: Judge - 1:6; 2:15; 3:1,2; 5:3,4

We search the Song in vain for the slightest judgmental word from the beloved. Nothing he said contributed to her malaise, and there is no criticism from him that could have made her feel bad. However, he is the writer of the Song, and he includes comments made by others, even those made by her. She was the one who divulged, "My mother's sons were angry with me," and she felt the heat of their blazing criticism implied by the word *nich͏aru* – from *chārar*, a burning anger. The New King James Version also attributes chapter 2:15 to her brothers – *"Catch us the foxes,"* and it is probably right, since the word *"us"* is plural, which in Hebrew means more than two. Evidently, they were concerned about their destructive behaviour that she wasn't able to address on her own, and so they determined to get rid of them. Foxes can be killing machines: they not only kill, but keep on killing until no chickens are left alive in a coop. They also kill lambs, and no doubt they would damage clusters of tender grapes, while their burrowing would have a bad effect on the vines.

Apart from her judgmental brothers, she had good reason for self-criticism. As we thought earlier, she depended on others to see, to find and to tell, yet had requested that he "Tell me." It shows how fickle the human heart can be: she wanted direct communication from him, yet thought indirect communication was all right from her. There was a lesson here for all Israel, including Dan, that their own relationship with God could bring criticism from others, and that a bit of healthy self-judgment wouldn't have been out of place. However, He expects that we tell Him ourselves about our relationship with Him, and that we don't rely on others doing it second-hand. Our relationship with the Lord Jesus Christ calls for real openness, even when we have to say, as she did, *"I sought him, but did not find him."* Her problem was, that she looked in the wrong places, and she should have been open with herself about this, too.

Dan made the same mistake. Living in the northern part of Israel, their king, Jeroboam, *"made two calves of gold, and said to the people, "It is too much for you to go up to Jerusalem. Here are your gods, O Israel, which brought you up out of the land of Egypt!" And he set one in Bethel, and the other he put in Dan."*[19] What an absurd and deeply offensive claim, even to suggest that lifeless gods had redeemed them! It sounds comparable with the Pharisees' claim in Matthew 12:24 that the Lord cast out demons by Beelzebub. Was this not the ideal time for Dan to have some serious self-judgment? It may well be, there are times when we need it in our own lives, too, especially if we try searching for Him in the wrong places or attempt serving Him in the wrong way.

*Asher: Happy, blessed - 6:9

Among the beloved's commendations of his bride, he included this: *"The daughters saw her and called her blessed."* In this lovely way, they drew on the word *āshar* from which Asher was given his name. When he was born, Leah said, *"I am happy, for the daughters of my people will call me blessed,"*[20] and, more than seven centuries later, the daughters said it of the Shulamite. Asher was suitably announced, as the blessing of his name was conferred on her, yet they often lived in much need of it themselves, and still do!

*Naphtali: My wrestling - 2:9,17; 8:14

While the bride gave ample evidence of things with which she wrestled that could have reminded the tribe of Naphtali of the meaning of their name, there is another reminder presented in the agility of the bridegroom. She had thought of him as *"a gazelle or a young stag,"* as he came leaping and skipping to see her. There was no dragging of his feet. It was at his dying father's bedside that Naphtali first heard the commendation, *"Naphtali is a deer let loose; he uses beautiful words,"*[21] and Solomon was a vivid reminder of both. For him, like the bounding deer, no barrier was too high to surmount, and he was a master of beautiful words. He never came with nothing to say, even when she gave him no answer. Nevertheless, her final words close the Song with the surmounting theme of Naphtali, *"Make haste, my beloved, and be like a gazelle or a young stag on the mountains of spices."* It's no longer the mountains of Bether's earlier separation,[22] but "of spices" – of the sweet fragrance of her beloved. And we would say, *"Amen. Even so, come, Lord Jesus!"*[23]

The day came when the greater Bridegroom came with something much more beautiful to say: *"Repent, for the kingdom of heaven is at hand."*[24] Eternity will reveal how many responded to the gospel from the tribe of Naphtali and have been included in the *"remnant according to the election of grace."*[25]

*Levi: Joined, united

As the Song comes to its end, all traces of separation are gone. Love has conquered all and it reaches its crescendo in their sense of belonging. Like Levi, they are attached to one another, joined in the bond of unity that God always longs to see from day to day in His people, and that always will be seen by Christ our Beloved as He delights in His bride, and as she delights in Him.

For What We Are Watching
It is not for a sign we are watching ...
For wonders above and below
The pouring out of vials of judgment,
The sounding of trumpets of woe;
It is not for a day we are looking
Nor even the time yet to be
When the earth shall be filled with God's glory
As the waters cover the sea;

It is not for a king we are longing
To make the world-kingdoms His own;
It is not for a judge who shall summon
The nations of earth to his throne.
Not for these, though we know they are coming;
They are but adjuncts of Him,
Before whom all glory is clouded,
Besides whom all splendour grows dim.

We wait for the Lord, our beloved,
Our Comforter, Master and Friend,

The substance of all that we hope for,
Beginning of faith and its end;
We watch for our Saviour and Bridegroom,
Who loved us and made us his own;
For Him we are looking and longing;
For Jesus and Jesus alone.
(Annie Johnson Flint)

13

CONCLUSION

"If I should find you outside,
I would ... I would ... I would."
(Song of Songs 8:1,2)

* * *

Hindsight has the potential to explain everything. Looking back over her journey, the bride could have given early voice to Solomon's yet unwritten words, *"Do not say, 'Why were the former days better than these?'"*[1] She may have felt this way at the beginning of chapter 1 when she was reflecting on whatever had preceded it, but not now. Relapse had turned to restoration, regret to repentance, and regress to renewal. In her new state of renewed thoughts, feelings and actions, she concluded that, even if they were to meet publicly outside, she would wish to show how refined her will, her walk and her work had become.

*"I would kiss you"

Knowing how modest she would have to be in hiding her feelings, she imagined how open she could be if he were one of her brothers with whom she could walk in public without being criticised or shamed. It's a word she uses three times: firstly, when thinking about walking openly with him, and twice in verse 7 where she drew twice from the little word *būz* to show how despised a man would be if he thought he could buy love. He would be *bōz yābūzū*– utterly despised and utterly scorned. Nevertheless, her real desire was to show him that her heart now felt unrestrained in its affection, that she was wholly his and holding nothing back.

*"I would lead you"

Loneliness was a thing of the past, and now she wanted to lose all sense of unaccompanied direction. She had known the shame of walking without him, and reaping the disapproval of watchmen and guardsmen. Now she wanted him to be welcomed into the place of her closest natural love-bond, "the house of her mother," like Isaac welcoming Rebekah into his mother Sarah's tent in Genesis 24:67.

*"I would cause you to drink"

She was the only cause of all that had gone wrong: their separation, and their sense of isolation. He had expressed his expectation of her in his sevenfold "my" in the first verse of chapter 5, but she gave her inadequate response in her tenfold "my" in the five verses that follow. Now she wants to be the means of unbroken communion and satisfaction, which must have delighted the heart of her beloved.

First things first

As we have thought at different stages of our journey through the Song, the fluctuations of the bride mirror the mercurial rise and fall of Israel's walk with God. The Song is His poetic heart voicing its longing for their return, to recapture what they had with Him in former days, and to make a similar threefold pledge of allegiance:

· No unrestrained affection;
· No unaccompanied direction;
· No more broken communion;

In days of their couldn't-care-less attitude toward Him, He could say, *"You have forgotten the God of your salvation, and have not been mindful of the Rock of your stronghold."*[2] By contrast, He said to them, *"O Israel, you will not be forgotten by Me!"*[3] Their forgetfulness was neither accidental nor unintentional, but the intended and inevitable result of not being intentionally mindful. Being mindful was a choice. Forgetfulness was a choice. And they still are! Either we hold to one and leave the other or we will leave the one and be taken hold of by the other!

At the beginning of Israel's journey, they saw the reality of redemption by the Passover lamb, and Psalm 106:9 speaks of their being led *"through the depths"* when the Red Sea parted. Of that time, verse 12 says, *"Then they believed His words; they sang His praise,"* but, before being taken into captivity in Babylon, they had neither faith nor song. As Jeremiah preached his God-given message, their hostility erupted in outright rejection, *"Let us not give heed to any of his words."*[4] Once again, it was their wilful rejection of God's Word that showed a deliberate choice not to be mindful of it or of Him, and forgetfulness followed. If only they had learned that His "depths" were higher than their heights![5]

A similar pattern unfolded in Ephesus, as we find in Revelation 2:1-7. The Lord's assessment of the church there appeared positive in its commendation until a single phrase brought it crashing down in condemnation: *"Nevertheless I have this against you."* It was a major change in direction, as He emphasised His on-going present view of their problem by saying, "I am having" or "I am holding." Evidently, they were a busy church, and we may take it as a compliment if He said to us, *"I know your works, your labor, your patience."* However, these can be viewed differently, once His complaint is attached to them. His short comment, *"You have left your first love,"* points to what was lacking in His seeming commendation.

Paul gave an almost identical commendation to the church in Thessalonica when he drew attention to their *"work of faith, labor of love, and patience of hope."*[6] He saw what the Lord didn't see in Ephesus, because an absence of *"first love"* meant their work was undermined by lack of faith, labour suffered from lack of love, and their sense of endurance was clouded by lack of hope. In other words, they were a mechanical or what we might call a clockwork church in perpetual motion. They were tireless in their doing, but had stopped being! They were clinically correct. They had remarkable ability to sift out the harmful and the heretic, testing them by the truth they held – as clear as the moon, but just as cold!

As far as the Lord was concerned, they needed to "Remember," which means, unlike Israel, they had to be mindful and not forgetful. Like Israel, they also needed to repent and restore. Having decided to leave their "first love," it wouldn't have taken long for "first works" to become a casualty, since being loveless leads to being fruitless. Just as *"faith without works is dead,"*[7] so work without faith is dead. "First love" for Jesus will lead to having "first works" for Jesus. It's all a matter of

'First things first'!

Overcoming or overcome?

Are overcomers normally in the minority? Like the Shulamite, Israel, and Ephesus, each of us has a decision to make in life: to overcome or be overcome. Both are in Scripture, but what does it take to be an overcomer? From the first use of the word "overcome" in Numbers 13:30, based on the word *yākōl*, we definitely get the impression that they are a minority group. Twelve men, hand-picked by Moses, had been sent to survey Canaan, to assess its population, its protection, its pasture and provision. By the meaning of their names, the spying mission looked as if it were in safe hands. From the first, Shammua meaning renowned, to the last, Geuel meaning the majesty of God, the enlisted men seemed an ideal selection.

We possibly could home in on Nahbi, whose name is linked to the occult, and think he may be the only fly in the ointment. However, there turned out to be ten flies, yet Caleb and Joshua stood out as overcomers among men who had been overcome. Caleb's assurance was *"we are well able to overcome,"* and his phrase consisted of twice using the same word – *yākōl nūkal* – as if to say, we are "well able well able" or we can "overcome overcome." Joshua supported him by drawing from Exodus 3:8 and stating, *"If the LORD delights in us, then He will bring us into this land and give it to us, 'a land which flows with milk and honey.'"*[8]

The secret of Caleb and Joshua's belief probably lay in the fact that God had already promised to do that. He also confirmed it in Ezekiel 20:6 – *"On that day I raised My hand in an oath to them, to bring them out of the land of Egypt into a land that I had searched out for them, 'flowing with milk and honey,' the glory of all lands."* When Moses urged the people in

Deuteronomy 1:21, *"Look, the LORD your God has set the land before you; go up and possess it,"* they insisted, *"Let us send men before us, and let them search out the land for us."* It was a mission doomed to fail, since it was based on assuming that they still needed to *"search out"* what God had already *"searched out"* for them! The lesson couldn't be clearer: overcoming is based on the word of faith; being overcome is the result of trying to do better without it!

John the Apostle fastened on this glorious truth in his first letter, chapter 5:4-5. *"For whatever is born of God overcomes the world. And this is the victory that has overcome the world— our faith. Who is he who overcomes the world, but he who believes that Jesus is the Son of God?"* This lies at the very foundation of each Christian's joy. He has said, *"I have overcome the world,"*[9] and His word *"overcome"* together with John's word for *"victory"* both come from the well know Greek word *nīkē*. So we are not working toward being overcomers; we are working from it. Nor do we gain the title by striving to be victorious; we are given the title by trusting the Victor!

The triumph is captured in the first occurrence of the word by what we would call the present continuous tense, which means that, in Christ, through the new birth, we continue to overcome the world. The second use of the word indicates that the state of overcoming continues because it has been granted through initial faith. The third indicates, similar to the first, that present and on-going overcoming go hand in hand with present and on-going believing. To put it in a nutshell, the new birth, and faith, guarantees that the gift of faith and accompanying victory are lifelong proofs of eternal salvation. There is mutual confirmation that those who are born again have overcome the world, and those who overcome the world are born again. One is the vital and vibrant proof of the other.

More than conquerors

As we know, the New Testament is full of teaching that exalts the Saviour and Romans 8 is within its treasury as an example of how the gospel of saving grace makes Christians *"more than conquerors."*[10] As it comes beaming to us through Paul's letter, our excited response can be like an echo of the bride, *"The voice of my Beloved! Behold, He comes leaping upon the mountains, skipping upon the hills."* As the Spirit of God caused him to show that the triumph of Christ has become the triumph of the Christian, He did something rather special. He took our little friend *nīkē* and stretched it out to become *hupernīkōmen* to emphasise that we don't merely overcome, but that we are over-overcomers. It's as if Paul became the messenger with Caleb's message, "We are well able to overcome." In such a wealthy chapter, it's easy to pick out good reason for this, such as verses 29 and 30:

> *"For whom He foreknew, He also predestined to be conformed to the image of His Son, that He might be the firstborn among many brethren. Moreover whom He predestined, these He also called; whom He called, these He also justified; and whom He justified, these He also glorified."*

He then thought of what the adversary might use to remove us from our security in God's eternal plan. He doesn't belittle the reality of such attempts, but it's as if he sets tribulation, distress, persecution, famine, nakedness, peril, and sword, like seven foothills lying below and dwarfed by the seven towering mountain summits of foreknowledge, predestination, being conformed to the image of His Son, Christ as firstborn and we as many brethren, being called, justified, and glorified. Earlier in the chapter, in verse 18, a similar contrast is made, *"that the sufferings of the present time are not worthy to be compared with the glory which will be revealed in us."*

If this wonderful chapter stands tall in all its grandeur of gospel exposition, and it does, chapter 12 should stand tall in our response to it. It opens with worship, and closes with a warning; with a call to respond to the call of God's goodness, and not to respond to the world's evil. It begins with an appeal to live the overcoming life, and ends with an admonition not to have our lives overcome. The chapter's final verse encapsulates the Christian's daily struggle: *"Do not be overcome by evil, but overcome evil with good."* In a very succinct manner, Paul puts the thought from the word *nīkē* into both phrases to show that there is an overcomer in each one of us, for evil or for good. He also shows in the twelve verses leading up to it that the possibility of being overcome begins in the church by:

- Not being hypocritical (v.9);
- To detest being harmful (v.9);
- Putting others first (v.10);
- Being generous to others (v.13);
- Not being high-minded (v.16);
- Not getting even or retaliating (v.19).

"even as I also overcame"

It may be as you read this that you are struggling and wondering if it will ever be possible to overcome and get your life spiritually back on track. If ever the Lord gave encouragement when recovery seemed least likely, it was to the church in Laodicea, which He described as *"wretched, miserable, poor, blind, and naked."*[11] Even so, He didn't write them off. He had a promise for them: *"To him who overcomes I will grant to sit with Me on My throne, as I also overcame and sat down with My Father on*

His throne." But how do we overcome? His answer still is, "as I also overcame." He is telling us to do it "as I" did it. There is no other way — "I" is our example, *"as"* is the manner of our example. He did it sacrificially, humbly, and obediently through His cross. It was the only way for Him, and it is the only way for us. *"If anyone desires to come after Me, let him deny himself, and take up his cross, and follow Me. For whoever desires to save his life will lose it, but whoever loses his life for My sake will find it."*[12] He lost His life for our sake, and overcame. Will we lose ours for His sake, and overcame?

> Must Jesus bear the cross alone,
> And all the world go free?
> No, there's a cross for everyone,
> And there's a cross for me.
> (Thomas Shepherd)

"I would ... I would ... I would"

God performs a most gracious wonder in human hearts and minds, in that He causes each believer who already thinks naturally to think biblically. 1 Corinthians 2:14 leaves us in no doubt that, *"The natural man does not receive the things of the Spirit of God, for they are foolishness to him; nor can he know them, because they are spiritually discerned."* This means, unbelievers can read the same portions of Scripture and be bewildered by them. Christians, meanwhile, learn that, while reading a book, such as the Song of Solomon, its meaning and relevance don't end with the last verse. As part of the overall canon of Scripture, it gives light to and receives light from other parts of God's inspired Word, and for this reason it pays to think biblically. He has deliberately used different ways of speaking to us: in history, in prophecy, in typology, in poetry, in imagery, in parables, in revelation, and in His Son.

The Song fills its own special place among the sixty-six books of our Bible, and holds its own special heart-warming appeal. In its own lovely way, we see the Lord Jesus Christ being portrayed, and gladly recognise Him as our Beloved, Bridegroom and King. The Shulamite's journey toward her beloved may in some ways reflect our own relationship with ours. Whoever she may have been, one thing is clear: while known to Solomon, she also was known by God. It's equally clear, since He has included her in His Word, that while she was moved by Solomon, she also was moved by Him. In this, she is no different from other brides like Rebekah and Ruth: they were women whom He called to fulfil His purpose, women who exalted Him, and were exalted by Him.

And still He calls, and asks if, like the bride, you will wholeheartedly surrender your affection, your direction, and communion. You can give your Beloved no better answer than the bride gave to hers, *"I would ... I would ... I would."*

OH, THE BITTER PAIN AND SORROW
Oh, the bitter shame and sorrow,
That a time could ever be,
When I let the Saviour's pity
Plead in vain, and proudly answered,
All of self and none of Thee.

Yet He found me; I beheld Him
Bleeding on the cursed tree;
Heard Him pray, Forgive them, Father,
And my wistful heart said faintly,
Some of self, and some of Thee.

Day by day His tender mercy,

Healing, helping, full and free,
Sweet and strong, and ah! so patient,
Brought me lower while I whispered,
Less of self, and more of Thee.

Higher than the highest heavens,
Deeper than the deepest sea,
Lord, Thy love at last hath conquered;
Grant me now my heart's petition,
None of self, and all of Thee.
(Theodore Monod)

* * *

"My beloved spoke, and said to me,
'Rise up, my love, my fair one, and come away.'
(Song of Songs 2:10)

REFERENCES

1 INTRODUCTION

(1) Jer.51:11 (2) Is.49:2 (3) Heb.1:3 (4) The Present Crisis by James Russell Lowell 1819-91 (5) Ex.10:21-23 (6) Ex.5:8-19 (7) Is.35:6 (8) Exploring Revelation by John Phillips, Kregel Publications (9) 2 Tim.3:16 (10) Rom.15:4 (11) Prov.14:10 (12) Song 1:3 (13) Jn 15:4 (14) Eph.5:1,2 (15) Col.2:9,10 (16) Is.53:12 (17) Phil.2:7 NASB (18) Ps.22:14 (19) Acts 10:45 (20) Titus 3:6 (21) Rom.5:5 (22) Song 2:5 (23) 1 Kin.4:33 (24) Jn 15:16; Gal.5:22,23; Heb.13:15 (25) Jn 15:2,5 (26) Heb. *mōr*: bitter (27) Heb. *kopher*: ransom, atonement, redemption price

2 THE SONG OF SONGS

(1) Deut.10:17; Jos.22:22; Ps.136:2; Dan.2:47; 11:36 (2) Eph.2:10 (3) Ps.115:4 (4) Prof. James Durham 1622-58, The Song of Solomon, page 42 (5) 2 Pet.1:21 (6) Eph.2:7 (7) Num.12:8 (8) 1 Sam.3:19 (9) Rev.2:4 (10) Col.3:2 KJV (11) Col.3:14 (12) 1 Chron.29:3 (13) Ps.51:15 (14) 1 Jn 4:19 (15) Jn 14:23,24 (16) Song 6:1 (17) Song 5:9 (18) 1 Pet.3:15 NIV (19) Song 5:11-16 (20) Song 1:4 (21) Jer.31:3; Hos.11:4; Jn 6:44; 12:32 (22) Jer.38:13 (23) Ps.85:8; 86:11 (24) e.g. Gen.48:12; Ex.6:26 (25) e.g. Gen.6:19 (26) Deut.6:23 (27) Song 1:2; 4:10 (28) 1 Jn 2:1; Jn 14:16; 2 Cor.1:3,4

3 SHADOWS

(1) Ps.23:1,2 (2) Matt.11:28 (3) Gen.38:14 (4) Jn 4:9,10 (5) Jn 10:3; 1 Pet.2:21 (6) Ps.100:3 (7) Ps.121:5 (8) Song 7:6 (9) Lk.1:79 (10) Eph.1:14 (11) Ps.34:8 (12) 1 Pet.2:3 (13) Gen.22:11; 46:2; Ex.3:4; 1 Sam.3:10; Lk.10:41; 22:31; Acts 9:4 (14) Gen.22:15; 1 Sam.18:21; Jer.33:1; Jonah 3:1; Hag.2:10,20 (15) 1 Sam.3:8; Matt.26:44; Jn 21:14,17 (16) Amos 6:12; Heb.12:11; Jas.3:18 (17) Heb.1:3 (18) Song 2:14; 5:2; 6:9 (19) Gen.8:7 (20) Ps.55:6-8 (21) Lev.1:14 (22) Lk.2:22-24 (23) Matt.3:16 (24) Song 2:14 (25) 1 Kin.4:33 (26) Ps.31:20 (27) Ps.32:7 (28) Is.32:2 (29) Is.32:3 (30) Zech.13:9 (31) Col.3:3 (32) 2 Sam.23:4 (33) Ps.102:11 (34) 1 Chron.29:15 (35) Amos 5:8 (36) Song 4:6 (37) see Matt.2:11; Mk.15:23; Jn 19:39 (38) Lev.2:1,2 (39) Heb.12:2 (40) Song 4:8 (41) Is.40:31

4 GLORY

(1) Lk.23:34 (2) Jn 19:27 (3) Lk.23:43 (4) Ps.69:21 (5) Acts 13:29 (6) Matt.6:28 (7) 1 Kin.7:21,22 RVM (8) Ps.19:3,4 (9) Rom.1:20 (10) Is.35:2 (11) Is.40:4,5 (12) 1 Sam.4:21 (13) Ex.29:43 (14) 1 Kin.8:11 (15) Is.43:21 (16) Acts 7:38 KJV (17) Song 8:5 (18) Mic.5:5 RV (19) Hos.14:4,5 (20) Is.46:13 (21) Jer.7:3 (22) Hag.1:5 (23) Jer.52:21 (24) Jn 1:18 (25) Jn 1:14 (26) Jn 2:11 (27) Jn 2:7,8 (28) Phil.2:7 NASB (29) Matt.17:2 (30) 1 Pet.4:13 (31) Heb.1:3 (32) 2 Pet.1:17,18 (33) Heb.2:9 (34) Heb.12:2 (35) Jn 17:4 (36) Ps.62:7 (37) 2 Cor.4:4 (38) Eph.1:18,19 (39) Rom.9:23 (40) Ex.33:18

5 WALLS

(1) Phil.2:3-5 (2) Eph.1:6 (3) Is.30:18 (4) Hos.14:4 (5) Ps.74:16 (6) Song 2:14 (7) Gal.3:2 (8) 1 Cor.1:26-29 (9) Heb.11:7 (10) Matt.28:20 (11) 2 Thess.1:11 (12) 1 Cor.15:58 (13) Lk.9:23 (14) Eph.6:13

6 HIS DESCRIPTION OF HER

(1) Is.11:2 (2) Jer.31:3 (3) Hos.11:8 (4) Hos.14:4 (5) Ps.27:4 (6) Matt.10:16 (7) Ps.115:5 (8) Rom.11:25 (9) Zech.12:10 (10) Judg.4:21,22 (11) Ezek.11:5 (12) 1 Chron.28:9 (13) Col.3:2 (14) Song 7:8 (15) Josh.2:18,21 (16) Ps.12:2-4 (17) Ps.45:2 (18) Prov.22:11 (19) Eph.4:29 (20) Col.4:6 (21) Ps.96:6 (22) Song 8:10

7 HER DESCRIPTION OF HIM

(1) Heb.10:5 (2) Is.53:3 (3) Lam.1:12 (4) Lk.23:35 (5) Is.44:21 (6) Ezek.16:4 (7) Heb.12:3 (8) Matt.17:2 (9) 1 Cor.2:8 (10) Jn 10:36 (11) Jn 19:12 (12) Heb.10:7 (13) Lk.22:42 (14) Jn 17:4 (15) Gen.33:13 (16) Is.53:7 (17) Matt.4:16 (18) Dan.7:9,13,14 (19) Mk.10:21 (20) Matt.9:36 (21) Lk.2:61 (22) Lk.22:32 (23) Lam.3:51 (24) Matt.26:67; Is.50:6 (25) 1 Pet.2:23 (26) Jn 7:43 (27) Lk.23:34 (28) Jn 19:26 (29) Lk.23:43 (30) Jn 19:28 (31) Acts 13:29 (32) Heb.13:15 (33) Song 7:8 (34) Gal.2:20 (35) 1 Tim.3:16 (36) Lk.23:46 (37) 1 Pet.2:21 (38) Is.53:6 (39) 1 Pet.2:24 (40) Ex.27:16 (41) Col.2:6,7

8 PRIESTLINESS

(1) Heb.2:9 (2) Hos.3:4,5 (3) Ps.48:12,13 (4) Is.62:6 (5) Lk.13:34 NASB (6) Jer.5:31 (7) Ps.80:8 (8) Hos.10:1 KJV (9) Is.19:3 (10) Jer.19:7 (11) Mk.11:13 (12) Is.5:1,3,4 (13) Is.1:5 (14) Ps.121:4-6 (15) Hos.11:8 (16) Prov.27:18 (17) Jn 1:48 (18) Lk.19:9,10 (19) Ex.3:8; Deut.26:9 (20) Ex.19:6 (21) Jn 10:28 NASB (22) 1 Kin.7:20 (23) 2 Cor.10:5 (24) Phil.4:7 (25) Heb.13:15 (26) Jer.18:18 (27) Ps.51:6 (28) Lev.2:14 RV (29) Deut.26:4

9 COMMUNION

(1) Ps.103:1 (2) Song 5:7,8 (3) Gal.2:20 (4) Jn 17:6 (5) Eph.1:13 (6) Song 2:10-17; 5:2-6 (7) Is.52:7; Rom.10:15 (8) Song 5:2 (9) Rev.3:20 (10) Jn 1:38,39 (11) Song 1:6 (12) Song 8:12 (13) Matt.7:3 (14) Song 2:10; 3:1,2; 5:5 (15) Rev.3:18 (16) Song 5:16

10 SEALS

(1) Ex.28:11,12,21 (2) Ex.28:28 KJV (3) Job 5:8 (4) Dan.1:8 (5) 2 Sam.7:10 (6) Deut.14:24 ESV (7) Acts 13:47 (8) Acts 13:48 (9) Jn 15:16 (10) Col.4:17 (11) Is.14:24,27 (12) Eph.3:11 (13) 2 Tim.1:9 (14) Rom.8:28 (15) 2 Cor.5:19 (16) 2 Tim.2:2 (17) 2 Cor.5:20 (18) Phil.1:17 KJV (19) Is.8:16 (20) Jn 6:27 (21) Rom.10:1,2 (22) Col.1:7, 4:12,13 (23) 1 Tim.4:6 (24) Gen.38:25 (25) Num.2:9 (26) Heb.7:14 (27) Hag.2:23 (28) Ezra 1:1-5 (29) Hag.1:14 (30) Hag.1:2,5,7; 2:15,17,18 (31) Zech.3:8; 6:12,13; 9:9; 13:7 (32) Hag.2:7 (33) Ps.22:14

11 JEHOVAH'S NAMES

(1) ASV, ESV, NASB, NASU, RV, Young's Literal Translation, Darby Bible (2) Gen.19:24; Lev.9:24 (3) Ps.107:2 (4) Is.5:1,7 (5) Jer.2:2 (6) Hos.1:1;2:7 (7) 1 Pet.1:8 (8) Jer.8:22 (9) Jer.17:14 (10) Song 1:7; 5:2 (11) Ps.121:4-6 (12) Gal.3:28 (13) Rom.12:5 (14) Num.23:21 (15) Jer.23:6 (16) Is.35:10 (17) Eph.1:6 (18) Rom.5:19 (19) Song 4:7 (20) Ex.12:5; 1 Pet.1:18,19 (21) Josh.5:12 ESV (22) Phil.4:19 (23) Eph.4:13 (24) Num.2:2 (25) Ps.60:4 (26) Num.1:52 (27) Col.3:15 ESV (28) Is.52:8 (29) Col.1:20 (30) Ezek.48:35 (31) Song 7:12 (32) Is.63:19 (33) Heb.12:14 (34) 1 Pet.3:15 NASB (35) Josh.5:13-15; Rev.19:14 (36) 2 Cor.2:14 (37) Jn 5:18

12 WALKING WITH HIM

(1) Hos.13:11 (2) Josh.14:2-4 (3) Josh.19:18 (4) Song 2:10,13; 4:8,16 (5) 1 Kin.8:13 KJV (6) 1 Sam.23:16 (7) Jer.29:13 (8) Is.52:8 (9) Hos.14:2 (10) Gen.30:11 (11) Gen.49:19 KJV (12) Col.1:5,6 (13) Gen.41:51 (14) Gen.50:20 (15) Is.59:20 (16) Gen.44:30 (17) Song 2:3 (18) Matt.24:30 (19) 1 Kin.12:28,29 (20) Gen.30:13 (21) Gen.49:21 (22) Song 2:17 (23) Rev.22:20 (24) Matt.4:13-17 (25) Rom.11:5

13 CONCLUSION

(1) Eccl.7:10 (2) Is.17:10 (3) Is.44:21 (4) Jer.18:18 (5) Jer.3:6 (6) 1 Thess.1:3 (7) Jas.2:6 (8) Num.14:8 (9) Jn.16:33 (10) Rom.8:37 (11) Rev.3:17 (12) Matt.16:24,25

MORE BOOKS BY ANDY MCILREE

Grace in First Peter - The Many-Splendoured Grace Shown to an Ungracious Man (Men God Moved - Book One)

As Andy says, "Tracing the grace of God in Peter's first letter is like seeing the glory of God in Romans and the greatness of God in Hebrews." In this deeply practical book, Andy takes us through each of Peter the rough fisherman's 5 chapters, and introduces us to the manifold grace of God expressed in at least 11 different aspects:

1. GRACE REQUIRED IN AN UNGRACIOUS MAN
2. GRACE RESTORED IN OUR MISTAKES
3. GRACE RECEIVED IN THE GOSPEL
4. GRACE REGARDED IN WORSHIP AND WITNESS
5. GRACE REINFORCED IN TRIALS
6. GRACE RECIPROCATED IN MARRIAGE
7. GRACE RECOGNISED IN HOLINESS
8. GRACE REVEALED IN SPIRITUAL GIFTS
9. GRACE REFLECTED IN LEADERSHIP
10. GRACE REGAINED IN BIBLICAL TRUTH
11. GRACE RE-EMPHASISED IN PAUL'S LETTERS

The Apostle Jude's Tripod - The Man, Method and Message of the New Testament's Forgotten Book (Men God Moved - Book Two)

The apostle Jude's little letter can easily be read within five minutes, yet it spans eternity past and future, history and prophecy, blessing and judgment, past revelation and fresh revelation, things known and not known, heaven's glory and hell's grief. And, like all Scripture, it has a God-given relevance for us in the present day:

* for reproof – showing when we are off track
* for correction – helping us to get back on track
* for instruction – enabling us to keep on track.

As Jude wrote his little book, it's as if he did so with the mindset of a surveyor, scanning the worrying spiritual landscape in front of him - 19 times in his short letter, Jude moves his surveyor's 'tripod' of threes to drive his point home. In addition to exploring each of these, Bible teacher Andy McIlree unpacks each verse across seven key themes of Salutation, Salvation, Contention, Condemnation, Revelation, Benediction and Doxology.

This is a very enlightening and practical study of a little understood, under-appreciated and often forgotten part of our New Testament.

Boaz - Ruth's Redeemer, Bridegroom and Lord of the Harvest (Men God Moved - Book Three)

The events of the book of Ruth are like a jewelled cameo woven into the fabric of Israel's chequered background. The account of Ruth's arrival on the pages of God's Word is an interweaving of His grace, His call – so typical of His reaching out to Abraham, Rahab, and to Gentiles – and His purpose. So, during Israel's dull days, she is like a colourful butterfly emerging from a very drab chrysalis.

There is no shallow end to the story of Ruth, as depths of despair at the beginning lead on to deepening delight, which causes us to exclaim, "Oh, the depth of the riches both of the wisdom and knowledge of God! How unsearchable are His judgments and His ways past finding out!"

Join Bible teacher Andy McIlree in this heart-warming study as, chapter by chapter, he explores the depths of this wonderful Old Testament book, and in particular how Boaz is a picture of the Lord Jesus as our kinsman-redeemer, bridegroom and the Lord of the harvest.

Seeing the Bride in All the Scriptures (Women God Moved - Book One)

After looking at Peter, Jude and Boaz as 'Men God Moved' who were stirred and carried along by the Holy Spirit to fulfil God's purpose, Andy turns to look at 'Women God Moved' to see how He also used them: some, by their godly example; others, because of the imagery conveyed by the place they occupy in His Word.

Along with everything God wants us to gain from this study, Christian women should be assured that He never devalues them. To prove this,

He has used a series of Bible brides to occupy very special places in His purpose, and emphasise that He elevates them to the highest possible level by using them as examples of what He calls "the bride, the Lamb's wife." Andy begins in Genesis and continue in the Books of the Law, before flowing on through the Psalms and the Prophets – and looks at Eve, Rebekah, Israel, the Shulamite, Ruth and more.

At the outset, Andy acknowledges that we have the right to explore the Word, but clear pictures will not emerge unless we give the Lord the right to explain. When He does, the effect on us ought to mirror how the two from Emmaus felt when they asked, "Did not our heart burn within us while He talked with us on the road, and while He opened the Scriptures to us?" May ours be the same!

The Five Solas of the Reformation

Five centuries after Luther nailed his Ninety-five Theses to the door of a Catholic church, is there still a need for reformation? Yes, the Reformers' 'Five Solas' – Scripture Alone, Christ Alone, Grace Alone, Faith Alone, the Glory of God Alone – should be engraved on all our hearts, and the need could hardly be greater for them to be nailed to the doors of today's shallow churches today that are in danger of "being destroyed for lack of knowledge" (Hosea 4:6).

Garments for Glory

This book is an indispensable in-depth study of the types and shadows (pictures) of Christ in Israel's High Priest under the Levitical Order of the Old Testament Tabernacle and Temple, and specifically how his work, person and clothing speak of Jesus as our Great High Priest on the throne of God. But this is far from a dry, scholarly endeavour; its meditations will make your heart soar in fresh appreciation of what God has so expertly revealed in His Word about His Son; and its challenges will help you consider afresh "how should we now live" in view of what God has revealed to us about His Son.

ABOUT THE AUTHOR

Andy was born in Glasgow, Scotland, He came to know the Lord in 1954, and was baptized in 1958. He is married to Anna, and he lives in Kilmacolm, Scotland. They have two daughters and one son. He entered into full-time service in 1976 with the churches of God (www.churchesofgod.info). He has engaged in an itinerant ministry in western countries and has been privileged to serve the Lord in India and Myanmar (formerly Burma).

ABOUT THE PUBLISHER

Hayes Press (www.hayespress.org) is a registered charity in the United Kingdom, whose primary mission is to disseminate the Word of God, mainly through literature. It is one of the largest distributors of gospel tracts and leaflets in the United Kingdom, with over 100 titles and many thousands dispatched annually. In addition to paperbacks and eBooks, Hayes Press also publishes Plus Eagles' Wings, a fun and educational Bible magazine for children, and Golden Bells, a popular daily Bible reading calendar in wall or desk formats.

If you would like to contact Hayes Press, there are a number of ways you can do so:

By mail: c/o The Barn, Flaxlands, Royal Wootton Bassett, Wiltshire, UK SN4 8DY

By phone: 01793 850598

By eMail: info@hayespress.org

via Facebook: www.facebook.com/hayespress.org

www.ingramcontent.com/pod-product-compliance
Lightning Source LLC
Chambersburg PA
CBHW072006040426
42447CB00009B/1515